A WEE GUIDE TO
The Picts

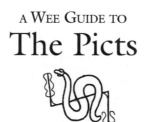

A WEE GUIDE TO
The Picts

Duncan Jones

GOBLINSHEAD
Musselburgh

A WEE GUIDE TO The Picts

First Published 1998, Reprinted 2000
Reprinted, updated and revised with some new illustrations 2003
Reprinted 2005 with minor revisions
Text © Duncan Jones 1998, 2003
© Martin Coventry 1998, 2003, 2005
Published by GOBLINSHEAD
130B Inveresk Road
Musselburgh EH21 7AY
Scotland

British Library Cataloguing in Publication Data
A catalogue record for this book is available from the British Library.
ISBN 1 899874 12 7
Typeset by GOBLINSHEAD using Desktop Publishing
Typeset in Garamond Narrow
Printed by Bell and Bain, Glasgow, Scotland

WEE GUIDES
Scottish History
Prehistoric Scotland
The Picts
Macbeth and Early Scotland
St Margaret and Malcolm Canmore
William Wallace
Robert the Bruce
Mary, Queen of Scots
Rob Roy MacGregor
Flora MacDonald
The Jacobites
Robert Burns
Whisky
Scottish Ghosts and Bogles

A WEE GUIDE TO
The Picts

Contents

List of illustrations

Acknowledgements

Many thanks to :

• **Tom Gray** for the permission to use the following illustrations
© T. E. Gray: Craw Stane, Rhynie (page 74), Rhynie Man stone (page 38),
Brechin Cathedral (page 44), Brodie Castle (page 45), Collessie (page
49), Dunfallandy (page 53), Elgin Cathedral (page 57), Edderton (page
58), Fowlis Wester (page 59), Inveravon Church (page 63), Rossie Priory
(page 75), Eagle Stone Strathpeffer (page 78), Raasay House (page 83).

• **Historic Scotland** for the permission to use the following illustrations
© Crown copyright: reproduced permission of Historic Scotland:
Aberlemno Stones (cover and pages 11, 40), Meigle Museum (frontis-
piece and page 68), Abernethy Round Tower (page 13); Abernethy Stone
(pages 15, 41); St Vigeans Museum (pages 76).

• **National Museums of Scotland** for the permission to use the
following illustrations
© The Trustees of the National Museums of Scotland 1998:
IB23 (page 15), IB22 - 1 (page 43), XIB 229 (page 50), IB36-4 (page 54),
IB189-7 (page 71), IB95 (page 80).

• **Groam House Museum & Pictish Centre** for the permission to use
the following illustrations
© S. E. Seright: Rosemarkie Cross (pages 62, 65).

Illustrations of Aberlemno roadside (page 1), Hadrian's Wall (page 4), St
John's Cross, Iona (page 8), Glamis Manse (page 35), Maiden Stone (page
47), Clach Ard (page 48), Eassie (page 56), Glamis Manse (page 61),
Kintore (page 66), Nigg (page 72), Shandwick (page 77), Sueno's Stone
(page 78) by Martin Coventry. Photo of Sueno's Stone (page 79) by Joyce
Miller. Symbol illustrations and Ogham alphabet (page 34) by Duncan
Jones. Maps and design by Martin Coventry.

Many of the sites listed are in the care of:
Historic Scotland (HS)
Longmore House, Salisbury Place, Edinburgh EH9 1SH
Tel: 0131 668 8800   Web: www.historic-scotland.gov.uk
The National Trust for Scotland (NTS)
Wemyss House, 28 Charlotte Square, Edinburgh EH2 4ET
Tel: 0131 243 9300   Web: www.nts.org.uk

How to use this book

This book is divided into three sections:

- The first part (pages 1-14) describes the history of the Picts, and there is a map of Pictish Scotland (page 2).
- The second part (page 15-34) looks at Pictish symbols, and is divided into rods, objects, abstract, animals and writing, and concludes with an Ogham alphabet (page 34). The common symbols are illustrated.
- The third part (pages 35-83) lists 135 symbol stones, museums and other sites which can be visited – although many are not open to the public and access should be confirmed before visiting. The section begins with a map (pages 36-7) which locates every site. The gazetteer is listed alphabetically (from page 39). Each entry begins with the name of the site and its reference on the map (pages 36-8), its location, then its National Grid Reference and Ordnance Sheet Landranger number where appropriate. Also included is the owner: Historic Scotland (HS); National Trust for Scotland (NTS). This is followed by a description of the site. The final part covers opening with telephone numbers and facilities, including parking (P), refreshments (R), sales area (S), admission charge (£), WC (WC), and disabled access. Further sites are listed (page 82).

An index (pages 84-6) lists all the sites, people and events alphabetically, and includes many cross-references.

Warning

While the information in this book was believed to be correct at time of going to press – and was checked, where possible, with the visitor attractions – opening times and facilities, or other information, may differ from that included. All information should be checked with the visitor attractions before embarking on any journey. Inclusion in the text is no indication whatsoever that a site is open to the public or that it should be visited.

The places listed to visit are only a personal selection of what is available in Scotland, and the inclusion or exclusion of a visitor attraction in the text should not be considered as a comment or judgement on that attraction.

Locations on the map are approximate.

Introduction

My first encounter with the Picts was in a field in Fife, sometime in the 1980s. I was looking at a standing stone when suddenly, as the sunlight slanted over the ancient surface, the incised outline of a warrior, armed with spear and shield, flicked into focus. One instant, nothing; the next, sun and shadow combined to bring this figure from the distant past into my view.

The Picts are the first people of Scottish History. They are the very earliest inhabitants of Scotland for whom we have any written material, although what we have is scarce to say the least. But we do have their most enduring legacy: their sculptured stones, carved and inscribed with an enigmatic symbolic language that defies our understanding to this day. The craftsmanship of these carvings fascinates me as much as their mysterious symbols. As pieces of history, as survivals of an ancient and vanished culture, the Pictish stones are indeed remarkable. As pieces of sculpture all are beautiful, and some are nothing short of works of art.

My thanks go to all those who have helped and encouraged me in writing this book, especially to the staff of the museums and visitor centres around Scotland who provided such patient assistance. Special thanks to Martin Coventry, Tom Gray, Fiona Guest, Alison Rae, John Smythe, Joseph White, Alison Green, Susan Seright and Joyce Miller.

DJ, Glasgow, May 1998

We have taken the opportunity to update visitor information, such as the opening of the Museum of Scotland, and also to add both Pictavia (an exciting attraction on the Picts) and Hilton of Cadboll, where Historic Scotland have placed a reproduction of the fabulous carved stone.

DJ, Glasgow, March 2003

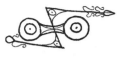

History of the Picts

Aberlemno

Map 1: Scotland of the Picts

History of the Picts

The Picts, their origin, language and society, remain to this day a topic of fierce debate in Scottish history. We have very little reliable information about them, and what written historical material we do have comes to us from sources outside the Pictish world – sources, moreover, that were hostile or at least unsympathetic to their culture, such as the Romans, the Scots and the Angles.

Who were the Picts? The first recorded mention of them comes from a Roman poem written in the late 3rd century AD, mentioning *Picti* and other barbarians. *Picti*, or 'Painted Men', was possibly the name given by the legionaries stationed on Hadrian's Wall to the tribes of the north, against whom they stood guard. However, it may have been a general term of abuse used by the Romans for any people from beyond the wild borders of their Empire; body-painting and tattooing was practised by many cultures, but was not a feature of life within the Empire and certainly not something which any true Roman would do.

This, perhaps, is the basic problem of the Picts – they were never conquered by the Roman Empire, and remained outside that great literate circle which might otherwise have recorded some of the details of their society. But the Romans did give the Picts something more than their name. Prior to the Roman approach, the northern tribes were small and fragmentary, occupied with petty feuds and rivalries, with no real concept of themselves as a people. It is likely that the presence to the south of a large, organised and foreign enemy helped these disparate tribes to coalesce into a more coherent group, at first for collective resistance and then into the beginnings of an early kingdom.

The first record of such an instance comes from the Roman historian Tacitus, describing the campaign of Agricola and his four legions beyond the Empire's northern border in the late 1st century AD. Central to his campaign was the defeat of a united army of tribesmen, collectively named Caledonians, in a battle at Mons Graupius. The location of this battle is unknown, but it has been suggested it was near Huntly in Aberdeenshire. The Caledonian tribes, led by one Calgacus, were heavily defeated by superior Roman weaponry, training and discipline, and Agricola completed his expedition without meeting further resistance. His supply fleet even sailed around the north of the country, locating the Orkney islands in the process. Tacitus was not unsympathetic to the Caledonian tribesmen; Calgacus is described as *a man of high courage and lineage*, and in his speech before the battle, wholly invented by Tacitus, he gives a ringing justification for resistance to the ever-expanding Roman Empire.

Despite Agricola's success, no attempts were made to conquer these northern lands, although it could be argued that they had no desire to acquire such a collection of forests and mountains. But the Romans certainly respected the men of the north as enemies; they built Hadrian's Wall, the largest piece of fortification in

Hadrian's Wall, Northumberland – built against the 'Picts' of northern Britain.

Western Europe, to keep them out. During their short-lived conquest of the lands up to the River Forth, they constructed yet another huge fortification, the Antonine Wall; and an entire Roman legion, the Ninth, having marched north into the lands of the tribesmen, simply vanished into the mists and forests – possibly of Galloway – never to return.

These tribesmen have been referred to as Proto-Pictish, hammered into co-operation by sporadic Roman incursions. By the 5th century AD and the Roman withdrawal from Britain, the major northern tribes had achieved some limited sense of unity, and were recognised, at least by outsiders, as one people: the Irish called them *Cruithni*, the 'People of the Designs'; others knew them as the Picts. It is not known what they called themselves. *Picti* may itself be an adaption of their own name, transformed by the Romans into a punning reference to their practice of painting or tattooing their bodies. Certainly *Pet* or *Pit* is a common feature of Pictish place-names – Pitlochry, Pitlessie, Pittenweem – and seems to refer to a unit of land; it is not improbable that they called their own land, and themselves, by some variation of that word. The element *Pent,* found both in the Pentland Hills and Pentland Firth, has also been suggested as an alternative name.

We do have some recorded versions of their own origin myths. One tells of a great warrior and king, Cruithne, who ruled over Alba – a name which can mean all of Britain or just the lands to the north of Hadrian's Wall – for one hundred years. He had seven sons, and after his death each son ruled over a portion of their father's kingdom. The names of these sons are still preserved today in some Scottish place-names: *Fib*, who ruled over Fife; *Cat*, who ruled Caithness; and *Fortriu*, who ruled the lands around the Forth. The other sons were *Fidach*, who held Moray; *Ce*, Aberdeenshire, Banff and Buchan; *Circenn*, Angus; and *Fotlaig*, Atholl and Strathearn. This legend, particularly since some of the names correspond to existing but undoubtedly ancient districts, probably gives us an idea of roughly how Pictland was divided. It also indicates that Strathclyde, Dumfries and Galloway and much of the Western Highlands were not part of Pictland at all. South-west Scotland was controlled by the British Kingdom of Strathclyde. The Western Highlands were peopled by the Scots, originally from the north of Ireland, who had been arriving there for centuries; in 500 AD, under King Fergus, they invaded Argyll and established the realm of Dalriada. Pictland proper, as indicated by place-name evidence and concentration of Pictish stones, appears to have been centred in the north and east of the country.

Other myths detailing the origins of the Picts survive. Ninnius, writing in the early 9th century, states that they arrived from the north, landing first in Orkney and then sweeping down across much of northern Britain. Ninnius may have been confusing the Picts with the first early appearances of the Vikings, since the Picts, like the Norsemen, raided by sea down the east coast of Britain. An Irish legend states that the Picts came from Scythia, near the Black Sea, and migrated up through Europe before arriving in Ireland, where they helped the Irish against their enemies. The Irish King helped them settle over the sea in Alba, giving them the widows of dead Irish warriors as their wives on condition that they always chose their kings from the female line.

This notion of a culture dominated by the female, rather than the male, line has proved attractive in recent years. Such societies have existed, and both archaeological and anthropological evidence exists to suggest a period in prehistory where matriarchal Earth-Mother-worshipping cultures were conquered or displaced by patriarchal Sun-God-worshipping ones. The idea that the Picts were a remnant of these Mother-Goddess societies, however, is highly suspect, and is part of one of the most pervasive myths surrounding the Picts: that they were some kind of lost people, an ancient survival of a prehistoric culture. If the Picts were a

matrilinear society, they would have been unique in Dark Age
western Europe. The only evidence to support this idea is a
throwaway comment in the Venerable Bede's *History of the
English Church and Peoples*, written in the 8th century AD, where
he repeats the Irish myth. This legend was particularly attractive to
the Dalriadan Scots, as it gave them a claim to kingship over the
Picts, and they probably repeated it at every opportunity.

The Picts were almost certainly a Celtic society of farmers and
hunters with many parallels to other cultures across northern
Europe. The Celts are a disparate group of peoples, sharing
common linguistic, social and artistic traits, who emerged from the
Near East during the Bronze Age around 1000 BC. They migrated
and conquered their way across Europe before being subsumed
into the Roman Empire (with the exception of the Irish and the
Caledonian tribes) before finally being swamped by the Germanic
invasions of Goths, Huns, Vandals, Franks, Angles, Saxons and
others in the first few centuries AD. Only Scotland, Ireland, Wales
and Brittany remained as a Celtic fringe.

Within that Celtic fringe is one major division, seen principally
in language. Celtic languages are divided into two groups:
Brythonic: Welsh, Cornish, Breton and the language of the ancient
Britons; and Goidelic: Scots and Irish Gaelic and Manx. What little
evidence we have of the Pictish language strongly suggests that it
was a Brythonic Celtic tongue: compare, for example, the number
of towns beginning *Aber-* (meaning a confluence or a river mouth)
in eastern Scotland with those in Wales.

Pictish society would have been similar in many important
aspects to other European barbarian cultures. Tribal in nature, it
would have been organised around a chief or chieftain who would
have had a retinue of elite warriors. They would have been
rewarded with honour, feasting and with moveable wealth,
ranging from gold and jewels to cattle and slaves, obtained by

raiding other communities. The poorer members of the community, unable to afford the weaponry or the leisure time of the warriors, would have occupied themselves with subsistence farming, paying small tributes to their chief and fighting only in desperate self-defence. With the withdrawal of the Romans and the growing organisation of the Picts, the opportunities for raiding increased enormously, and successful chiefs began to build on established power-bases. Occasionally, one chief might become powerful enough to exact tribute from his neighbours, along with an acknowledgement of superiority, and the notion of a High King – perhaps as overlord, perhaps simply first among equals – would develop.

St John's Cross, Iona – the doorway leads to the 9th-century St Columba's shrine.

Pictland was becoming more cohesive, with power centralised in the persons of chiefs and kings. The arrival of Christianity spurred things on even further. The Christian church was an enormous force for the organisation of a kingdom; a literate clergy could form a basis for an administration, whilst their theology helped to justify and confirm royal power. The most famous missionary to the Picts was St Columba, an Irish monk of noble blood, who travelled from Iona up the Great Glen to the palace of the powerful Pictish king, Bridei (or Brude) near Inverness or possibly at Urquhart. According to St Adamnan, Columba's hagiographer, he had a magical duel with Bridei's chief magician, Broichan. St

Columba was naturally victorious, and even cowed the fearsome kelpie, or water-horse, which inhabited Loch Ness. In reality, all that Columba achieved was the opening up of northern Pictland to Christian missionaries, and the acquisition of the island of Iona as a monastic centre.

Christianity also spread into Pictland from the south. St Ninian, based at Whithorn in the British kingdom of Strathclyde, St Kentigern (or Mungo) and St Rule all made incursions into pagan Pictland from the 5th century onwards. Although 'conversion' is probably too strong a word for what they achieved – most of the population would have continued to practise the beliefs and customs of their ancestors – gradually the new religion spread and absorbed or displaced the old.

The struggle for power in these kingdoms, however, went on between the northern Picts, their southern kinsfolk, the Dalriadan Scots and the Britons of Strathclyde and Lothian. New enemies were emerging, too. The lands south of Hadrian's Wall had fallen to the invading Saxons and Angles, and it was the latter, from Northumberland in particular, who were to prove the most threatening. From the late 6th century, the power of the Kingdom of Northumbria had been growing steadily. In 603 AD, alarmed at their expansive and aggressive nature, King Aedan of Dalriada mounted an invasion of their territory.

Aedan was a good example of the kind of king emerging from the northern lands. He was Scottish in ancestry, and had fought for many years with his Pictish neighbours, although he married a Pictish princess, marking the way forward for the coming together of the two peoples. Marching south with his allies from Strathclyde, and doubtless from Pictland as well, he met the Northumbrians in battle at Degastan. The result was a resounding victory for the Angles; two of Aedan's sons were killed, his army was destroyed and Aedan himself disappeared from history.

Degastan marked the beginning of Northumbrian expansion

northwards, and the immediate losers were the Britons of Lothian and the southern Picts. Between around 657 AD and 685 AD much of southern Pictland was occupied by the Angles, then at the height of their power. The occupation was hated by the Picts, who attempted rebellion more than once. The Angles even installed their own bishops, and it looked as if much of Pictland would be forever absorbed into a greater Northumbria.

But one man emerged who was to have as much influence on the future course of history as Robert the Bruce: Bridei, grandson of King Neithon of Strathclyde – not to be confused with King Bridei who received St Columba. Bridei's campaign began around 680 AD, when he conquered and brought under his control the northern Pictish lands. By 683 AD he had subdued the Scots, even besieging and assaulting their capital at Dunadd in Argyll. A strong and determined ruler, his ultimate aim was achieved in 685 AD when he brought the Northumbrians to battle at Nechtansmere – also known as Dunnichen – near Forfar in Angus.

Nechtansmere ranks alongside Bannockburn as a decisive battle which shaped the destiny of an entire country, for without it there is every chance that the later kingdom and nation of Scotland would never have existed. Bridei knew the power of the Northumbrians; he also knew that they were supremely confident and despised their northern enemies. Playing on their arrogance, he lured their army northwards into hilly, broken terrain where their superior strength and numbers were of limited value. Dividing his army in two, he sent the weaker half forward to confront the enemy, keeping the bulk of his troops in hiding behind Dunnichen hill. After a short engagement, the weaker Picts withdrew back over the hill. The exultant Angles broke ranks and pursued them, only to come face to face with the main Pictish force, formed up in battle array. Trapped by the Picts, with no escape except through the marshy terrain at the foot of the hill, the Northumbrians were defeated with great slaughter. Their King,

Egfrid, and his retinue were all killed. The power of the Northumbrian kingdom was broken forever, beginning a long slow decline until it was absorbed into the emerging kingdom of England.

Bridei's momentous victory is recorded in stone on the beautiful cross-slab in Aberlemno

Aberlemno churchyard – said to commemorate the victory of the Picts over the Angles at the battle of Nechtansmere in 685.

churchyard, a few miles from the site of the battle. It marked the beginning of a period of ascendancy for Pictland, united now under one ruler. Several other kings followed Bridei after his death in 693 AD, and although Northumbria continued to be a threat, it was the Dalriadan Scots who were now seen as the greatest menace. Perhaps the most obvious sign of this comes from the reign of Nechtan Mac Derile, who ruled from 706 AD to 724 AD. Perceiving that, since Nechtansmere, the Irish churchmen – many with strong connections with the Scots – had gained a disturbing amount of influence in his realm, he adopted the practices of the

Northumbrian church and expelled the Columban monks to the west of the country.

Nechtan was a religious man, and eventually resigned his kingship and became a monk. Out of the confused struggle for power, following his abdication, emerged a new dynasty, founded by Oengus Mac Fergus. Oengus was a violent and energetic man who ruled from 731 AD to 761 AD; he crushed his enemies, executed the King of Atholl by drowning, captured Dunadd, conquered Dalriada and became the first king of both Picts and

Dumbarton Rock – ancient fortress of the Britons of Strathclyde. It was besieged by the Picts in 756.

Scots. His expanding ambitions foundered finally on the rock of Dumbarton as he tried, with Northumbrian help, to add the Kingdom of Strathclyde to his possessions in 756 AD.

Oengus died in 761 AD, and with him died the union of Pictland and Dalriada. Under King Aed, the Scots threw off Pictish rule and once more asserted their independence. But the idea of a united kingdom had been born, and was realised again under Constantine Mac Fergus, who ruled Pictland from around 789 AD to 820 AD. His son, Donald, became King of Dalriada, and on his death in 811 AD Constantine gained his son's throne as well.

After Constantine's death the kingdoms again split apart, and a series of generally short-lived kings followed him. However, it must be appreciated that, by this time, intermarriage, particularly among the royal and aristocratic families, had made the Pictish and

Scottish rulers almost interchangeable, and a unification under one royal house could be seen as inevitable.

The final pressure for union came from outside, in the form of the Vikings. What began as a trickle of Norse trader-pirates turned into an annual flood of raiders and settlers, and in 839 AD a united army of Picts and Scots was destroyed by the Vikings. Neither kingdom could exist in isolation any more. The Picts, on the east, were in the direct line of attack, and the Dalriadan Scots were cut off from their Irish cousins. Chance, more than anything else, determined which kingdom and culture would dominate.

Kenneth Mac Alpin, King of Dalriada, was the one to snatch the prize, and in 842 AD he moved his court to the ancient Pictish royal centre at Scone. From Dunadd he brought the Stone of Destiny, an ancient artifact used in the inauguration of Scottish Kings, now kept in Edinburgh Castle. Legend states that he invited the Pictish nobles to a feast before treacherously massacring them, although this is probably untrue; the Pictish nobility had already

Round tower, Abernethy – this was an important Pictish site.

13

been decimated in battle by the Vikings. Although there was some resistance, by 848 AD Kenneth Mac Alpin had become the first true King of Scots – a name which must now be expanded to include the Picts as well. By moving the centre of his royal power, by diplomacy, force of personality and of arms, and by providing a single rallying point against the Norse invaders, Kenneth Mac Alpin did more than merely rule two kingdoms; he made them into one.

From this point on, Pictish language and culture declined. Gaelic was the language of the court and of the new ruling class, and of the resurgent Columban church. But the court was established in Pictish territory, in important royal centres such as Scone, Dunkeld, Abernethy and Dunfermline, and the Pictish ecclesiastical centre at St Andrews became the pre-eminent bishopric in all of Scotland. Indeed, the old Scottish power-base in Argyll and the Western Highlands drifted out of royal control, some parts of which never fully returned until the modern era, and it was the Pictish heartlands which became the foundations of the Scottish nation. Although the Picts are lost to history, they have never truly gone away. Their legacy in stone is still with us.

Pictish symbols

Myreton – the Pictish symbol stone known as the Picardy Stone

Pictish symbols

In examining all the various Pictish designs and
carvings, it is important to bear in mind the
difference between pictures – straightforward
depictions of animals, people and things, and
symbols – designs with inherent meanings of
their own. The difference between a picture and a symbol is one of
context: an eagle shown as part of a hunting scene is a picture,
whereas an eagle shown by itself is deemed to be a symbol. Of
course, an eagle in a hunting scene may still have as much
symbolic meaning as an eagle carved alone – much of the
interpretation of Pictish art is fraught with problems like this.

Sometimes these symbols are recognisable as objects in their
own right, and sometimes they are either heavily stylised or
entirely abstract. Modern road-signs use a similar combination of
the realistic and the symbolic. The *Men at Work* sign is an obvious
depiction of a man shovelling; the *Crossroads* sign is a stylised but
recognisable diagram of a crossroads, although shown not as one
would see it from the road but from overhead; and the *No Entry*
sign – a white horizontal bar across a red circle – is wholly
abstract. With a bit of imagination and common sense – especially
if they knew the symbols were road-signs – future archaeologists
could make a decent attempt at figuring out the meanings of the
first two, but, without a copy of the *Highway Code*, what would
they make of the third?

Unfortunately, we do not have a Pictish *Highway Code* to help
us, and in any case, the symbolic language of their stones is far
more complex than that of modern traffic signs. We do not even
know what they were for; did they represent boundary markers,
memorials, decrees or shrines, or did they have some other,
forgotten purpose? Many stones may have had more than one
function. The designs themselves may have possessed more than
one meaning, depending on their context. It has even been

suggested that these symbols, frequently found in pairs, represented syllables in the Pictish language, spelling out names of Pictish warriors, chieftains and kings. Some, none or all of these interpretations may be true: it is entirely possible that, as in so many symbolic languages, one interpretation lay on top of other, deeper meanings, perhaps religious, perhaps jokes or puns, or all at once.

Many symbols are widely distributed across Scotland, and appear everywhere from beautiful shaped and carved stones to scratchings on cave walls. Whatever their meaning, the Pictish symbols were widely understood by the people who made them. In an almost wholly illiterate society, the language of symbols becomes even more important. Depictions of certain things, places or people become conventionalised. In medieval Christian art, for example, the symbols of the saints were the same across Europe: St James the Greater had a scallop shell; St Peter the keys to Heaven, and so on. Matthew, Mark, Luke and John – the four Evangelists – were routinely symbolised as a man, a lion, a calf or bull and an eagle respectively, from Ireland to Constantinople. Other, more obscure symbols abound: the lily in a vase representing the Annunciation, or the rose representing Christ's Passion. Even in the modern world, symbols from the past are still in use; the striped barber's pole, for example, or the three balls hanging outside a pawnbroker's. In the descriptions of the Pictish symbols that follow, sensible interpretations have been attempted, where possible, based on what little is known about the Picts and their culture. But one important fact to stress is this: nobody knows for sure. The reader may disagree with some or all of the conclusions in this book – and may well be right.

Conventionally, Pictish stones are divided into three classes. **Class 1** stones are natural rocks or boulders containing groups – usually pairs – of incised symbols. Many Class 1 stones appear to be much earlier Bronze or Stone Age monoliths, which the Picts later decorated with their own designs. None of these stones carry any recognisable Christian images. Although many were doubtless carved before the arrival of St Columba, Class 1 stones continued to be made well into the Christian era.

Class 2 stones are shaped and dressed, usually carved in relief – that is, with the figures raised up out from the background – and carrying Christian symbols. These are almost always cross-slabs, although some are in the form of altars or stone boxes. Class 2 stones also carry many of the symbols found on Class 1 stones.

Class 3 stones are similar to Class 2, but carry no Class 1 symbols.

The Pictish symbols have been variously interpreted as representing tribes, gods, saints, professions, ranks, natural forces, seasons or various combinations of these and other possible meanings. There is as yet no agreed system of names for all the various designs: one person's 'tuning fork' is another's 'broken sword', so names have been used which are the least misleading in order not to get too obsessed with identifying what all the designs actually represent. The symbols have been divided into four separate types: the **Rods** – v-, z- and straight; **Objects** – more or less recognisable items from everyday life; **Abstract** – shapes which, while they may represent actual items, are not readily identifiable as such; and **Animals** – both real and fantastic birds, beasts and fish.

Of course, there are many Pictish carvings which do not fit into these categories. Essentially, any design which is recognisably repeated elsewhere has been considered a symbol. Even when it is unique, if its prominence and lack of other associations – such as the stag on the stone from Grantown on Spey, now in the **Museum of Scotland** in Edinburgh – show it to be important in its own right rather than part of a larger scene, it has been accepted as a symbol. Some other unique designs – such as the ferocious Rhynie man, now in the offices of the **Aberdeenshire**

Council – it was decided not to choose to identify these as symbols, seeing them rather as illustrations of characters out of mythology. Rhynie man, with his jagged bared teeth and outsize features, looks like a giant: perhaps Goliath, perhaps one of the many giants from folklore. Whilst he may have symbolic connotations, he does not seem to belong to the alphabet of a Pictish symbol language. In all, care has been used in identifying symbols as opposed to pictures, and where there was any doubt it was chosen to err on the side of caution.

RODS

The rods are always found in association with other symbols, never simply by themselves, and may therefore be some kind of qualifier such as 'Great', 'Royal', 'Holy', 'Dead' or some other adjective. They may of course have other, more subtle, connotations. Most of the rods seem to have definite heads – usually arrow- or spear-shaped – and tails, although with some there seems to be no obvious distinction. These may simply be artistic embellishments, or they may hold further refinements of meaning in their orientation and direction.

Straight rod

Very rare, and only ever found crossing the snake symbol. Because of the association of the snake symbol with the z-rod, the straight rod may represent a variant, or even an abbreviation, of the z-rod.

V-rod

Almost every crescent is found crossed with a v-rod, and this rod is not associated with any other symbol, except once: the **Migvie** cross-slab has an arch with a v-rod, although it is just possible that this arch is a variant of a crescent.

Interpretations range from a broken arrow to a depiction of the rising and setting of the sun and/or moon.

Z-rod

Found crossing the snake, the double disc and the notched rectangle, the z-rod has been seen as a broken spear symbolising death, or possibly martial prowess.

Many carvings, such as the **Collessie** stone, **Dupplin** cross or the **Aberlemno** churchyard stone, seem to indicate that the stabbing-spear, rather than the sword, was

the pre-eminent Pictish weapon. The z-rod could indeed represent one whose spear was broken – dead – or one who was a breaker of spears – a great warrior. Another interpretation could be a thunderbolt, representing a sky-god such as Taranis, the Celtic god of thunder.

OBJECTS

Anvil (?)

This has been tentatively identified as an anvil, mainly because it has appeared in association with the hammer and tongs – for example, on the back of the **Dunfallandy** cross-slab. Thus it could represent ironworking and the blacksmith's trade, a profession with many deep connections to mythology and folklore. Some of the *anvils*, however – like the one on the slab at

the foot of the **Abernethy** round tower – bear more than a passing resemblance to much earlier Bronze Age axe-head designs.

Cauldron (?)

Again, this is a fairly tentative identification. The cauldron here is viewed from above: the central circle represents its mouth, the cauldron being hung over the fire from the two side rings. The picture is perhaps clearer where the artist has carved a central bar running through the side rings, although this is not always shown. It could be argued that this is a peculiar way to represent a cauldron; indeed, a cauldron – with two pairs of human legs waving out the top – is shown in a more conventional side view on the **Glamis Manse** stone, opposite a much larger triple-circle symbol. Cauldrons are very important in Celtic mythology, being associated with healing and rebirth, as well as

magically inexhaustible sources of food. Two Celtic deities, Dagda the Good and the goddess Ceridwen, are both connected to such miraculous vessels, and the Christian Church adopted and adapted the Celtic cauldron in the form of the Holy Grail. Also, a cauldron could represent generosity, an extremely important virtue for a king or warrior, showing the ability to feed many followers.

Hammer

As with the anvil, there are obvious associations with blacksmiths and metalworking in general.

Mirror & Comb

This paired symbol – although on occasion the mirror is portrayed alone, without the comb – is frequently taken to represent a woman, and indeed the mirror and comb were common symbols in the ancient world of one aspect of the Mother Goddess. In Celtic societies, however, men were deeply conscious of their personal appearance, and took great care with their apparel and especially their hair. Classical sources often mention the elaborate hairstyles of the Celts – so different from the severe Roman short-back-and-sides – which

they braided and held in place with combs and other ornaments. Bone combs, which were intricate constructions in themselves, made of several interlocked pieces, were often placed in graves along with other necessities for the afterlife, and were sometimes part of the regalia of bishops and other churchmen. Mirrors and combs also have magical connotations, and often appear in folklore as enchanted objects.

Shears

These are quite obviously different from tongs and bear a close resemblance to the implements used for shearing sheep up to the advent of modern electric clippers. This may be what they represent, although there could be a punning reference to Christian monks, with their shorn heads, croziers and flocks.

Tongs

Again, like the hammer and anvil, the most obvious connection is with metalworking. They are often found in association with one or both of these other symbols.

ABSTRACT

Arch

Sometimes decorated, sometimes plain, this has been seen as a horseshoe (although no Pictish horseshoes have ever been found), a rainbow, or a sword-chape: the metal tip of a scabbard. In one instance – on the **Migvie** cross-slab – an arch is crossed with a v-rod, perhaps indicating some sort of connection with the crescent.

Bow and Arrow (?)

This appears only once, on one of two incised stones at **Congash** Farm near Grantown on Spey. It has also been interpreted as a helmet with an ornamental nose-guard, but it is most probably neither.

Crescent

The crescent is almost always crossed with a v-rod, and is often elaborately decorated. There are obvious lunar associations, although it could also perhaps be seen as representing the dome of the sky – certainly it is most frequently found in the orientation illustrated here. This is by far the most common of all the Pictish

symbols, appearing over 100 times – 80% of the time with a v-rod – and we can be sure that its frequency indicates its importance. One striking example, now lost, was a bronze crescent-shaped plaque found at Monifieth Laws in Angus. 114 mm (4.5 inches) across, it was decorated with a v-rod on the front and a double disc and z-rod on the back. Although it is not clear what this plaque was for, or what it represented, it was obviously highly prized: a later (probably Viking) owner had his name engraved in runes on one side.

Double Crescent

An uncommon symbol. It may be a variation on the single crescent.

Double Disc

A relatively common symbol, especially when crossed by a z-rod: approximately 70% of all double disc symbols have z-rods. It has been imaginatively interpreted as a torque, an armlet made of

twisted metal rods with flared, trumpet-like ends, seen side on –
the two discs are the end-pieces and the connecting lines
represent the connecting rods, curving out behind. This seems
unlikely: it would take a very peculiar kind
of artist to draw a C-shaped piece of
jewellery in this way. Moreover, other
similar double disc symbols have been
found in examples of Celtic art from across Europe, frequently in
association with religious imagery. Perhaps it represents the two
worlds: the here-and-now and the 'otherworld'; life and death.
Several examples look suspiciously like two single disc and
rectangle symbols joined together. Perhaps the double disc
signifies another sort of union – the marriage of two families?

Flower

The name of this symbol derives from its vaguely plant-like shape.
It could equally represent a tree – although
perfectly recognisable trees are carved on other
stones – or a spring. It has also been compared to
a horse ornament. On one of the Golspie stones in
the **Dunrobin Museum**, showing a crowded
scene including a bearded warrior armed with a
knife and a battle-axe, the warrior's outstretched
foot is touching a 'flower' which looks almost like a fortress,
perhaps with smoke and flames issuing from the top.

Knot

This is a piece of Celtic interlace art in isolation. It
only appears on Class 2 stones, so it may be a
triquetra, a Christian symbol representing the Holy
Trinity.

L shape

Indecipherable. This symbol may have a connection to the stepped rectangle.

Notched Rectangle

This symbol is almost always combined with a z-rod: the only two exceptions at present are in the **East Wemyss Caves** in Fife and on the fastening of a Pictish silver chain, now in the **Museum of Scotland** in Edinburgh. The opposing circular notches are a common feature. It has been tentatively identified as a chariot, seen from above, pulled by two ponies. Others see it as representing a fortress or a gateway.

Rectangle

The most obvious suggestion for this symbol is a chest or box of some description, or a rectangular shield. Some examples, however, have asymmetric designs within the rectangle that seem to represent a pouch or satchel, perhaps for carrying a Bible. One of the Golspie stones in the **Dunrobin Museum** looks particularly like a satchel with a fastener.

S-shape (1)

This has a suggestion of an edged implement – perhaps a razor – although this is pure speculation. An uncommon symbol, so far it has been found only four times.

S-shape (2)

This symbol appears only twice. One suggested interpretation is a seal, but, since all the other Pictish representations of animals are realistic and instantly recognisable, why should their seals be so abstract? It does, perhaps, have a certain marine flippered appearance.

Single Disc and Rectangle

Also described as a 'mirror case', this has been seen as representing either a round-house, a burial mound or a sun-symbol. When it appears with the bottom of the rectangle notched, it has also been interpreted as a human figure holding up a solar disc – the notch represents the legs. It also bears a passing resemblance to one half of a double disc.

Square with Corner Decoration

This has only appeared once so far; it may be purely decorative.

Stepped Rectangle

Indecipherable.

Three Circles in One

This appears seven times, six times on Class 1 stones – therefore it is probably not a symbol of the Christian Trinity. However, the pagan Celtic religion had a trinity of its own – the triple-aspect Goddess – and this may be what is represented here.

Three Ovals

Not a common symbol, this has been seen as representing a spiral bracelet or some other decoration. It is, however, a triple symbol and, although not common, may represent either the Celtic Trinity (on Class 1 stones) or the Christian Trinity (on Class 2).

Tuning Fork

The name of this symbol derives purely from its shape – the Dark Age Picts did not have tuning forks. It has been interpreted as a broken sword or a pair of tongs – but it does not look like either. This is one of the most frustrating Abstract symbols: it looks like a realistic depiction of an actual item – something with a handle and two long prongs – but no such item has ever been found and it has never been convincingly identified. Possibly it represents a tool whose purpose is now long-forgotten, or a ceremonial staff of office. If the 'handle' does in fact represent a grip for one hand, then the prongs of the 'tuning fork' would have been about 600 mm (24 inches) long.

ANIMALS

Animal symbols, as opposed to pictures of animals, have been seen as representing tribes or at least prominent families. It is not uncommon for tribal societies to identify themselves with totem animals. One major branch of the Picts were called *Cat* or *Cait*, meaning 'Cat People', a name which is preserved today in Caithness. No Pictish art, however, has been found depicting a cat in anything like the realistic style of other animal carvings. As well as the usual collection of possible meanings, animal symbols may also allude to actual or perceived qualities of the animals themselves.

Boar

There are only four known Pictish boar symbols, although this animal was extremely important in Celtic mythology and the boar-hunt was a common – and dangerous – aristocratic pastime. Pigs in general were associated with magic and the 'otherworld', and many legends deal with transformations

from pigs to people, and vice versa. The boar would represent strength, cunning and ferocity. A boar's head is a common feature of many Scottish coats of arms. One carving is found at **Dunadd**.

Bull

Commonly representing power, strength and fertility, the bull was often associated with the sea as well. There is also a Christian link with the Evangelist St Luke. Numerous carvings of bulls have been found, in particular at **Burghead** on the Moray coast, the site of a powerful Pictish harbour and sea-fort. Cattle were also one of the principal forms of wealth.

Eagle

In Christian iconography, the eagle represents St John the Evangelist. Celtic folklore portrays the eagle as King of the Birds. In Scottish heraldry, eagle feathers are the mark of chieftainship – perhaps the same symbolism is intended here.

Goose

Many stories tell of the vigilance of this bird. Rome is said to have been saved from barbarian assault when the sentries were alerted by the cackling of geese. Certainly geese – loud, aggressive and easily disturbed – make excellent burglar alarms and night-time guardians. This Pictish goose, looking alertly over its shoulder, has the air of a watchful sentry. Moreover, Julius Caesar's account of the ancient Britons states that, to them, the goose was a sacred animal. Perhaps the Picts, like their southern neighbours, held the bird in similar regard.

Horse

Although the horse appears only once on its own in Pictish art (on one of four carved stones in **Inverurie Old Churchyard**), many larger scenes show mounted warriors or hunters. The horse was a very important cult animal to Celtic societies across Europe, representing Epona, the Horse Goddess. Associated with power and nobility, the horse could also  represent the gift of prophecy and act as a messenger from, and a link to, the 'otherworld'.

Pictish Beast

All the Pictish symbol-creatures represent actual animals, drawn with great skill, evoking the feel of moving, living beasts. What, then, are we to make of the Pictish beast, which alone makes up some 40% of all the animal symbols yet found? It is carved in the same style as all the rest, and its form is repeated on stones across Scotland, yet it resembles no known animal. It has been called a 'swimming elephant', and compared to a dolphin or a whale, but since all the other animals are accurately observed and realistically portrayed, why is this creature so hard to identify? Obviously, any symbol so  common and so widespread must have been of great importance, but it seems unlikely it represents a real animal – certainly no more than the unicorn supporters of the Royal Arms of Scotland. This is a Pictish dragon, or some other powerful mythological creature. With its flipper-like limbs, it does have an aquatic appearance: perhaps, then, it represents a kelpie or water-horse, like the famous denizen of Loch Ness – from whose jaws St Columba saved a man – or one of the dozens of others which are said to haunt many a Highland loch. In fact, perhaps it was a sacred pagan symbol, and the story of St Columba's triumph is not the earliest recorded sighting of Nessie but a metaphor for the subjugation of the old religion by the new.

Salmon

The salmon is the second most common animal figure, just ahead of the snake. A fish has been a sign of Christianity since earliest times, and some of that symbolism may be present in the salmon carved on Class 2 stones. But this is not just a fish: this is very  definitely an accurate portrayal of a salmon. Many folk-stories refer to salmon, and they were often seen to represent knowledge and the power of prophecy.

Snake

One of the most common animal symbols, the snake is often crossed by a z-rod, and occasionally by a straight rod – the only animal symbol found associated with any of the rods. Because it is so common, and because it is the only natural figure to be crossed with any of the rods, the snake was obviously an extremely important symbol. Across the world, snakes and  serpents are associated with magic, with death and rebirth, with sex and healing. Only that other magical animal, the salmon, and the mysterious Pictish beast appear more often than the snake.

Stag

Deer in general, and stags in particular, have always been important in the mythologies of European societies. It is perhaps surprising that only one stag symbol has been found to date, on the Grantown on Spey stone, now in the

Museum of Scotland in Edinburgh. Cernunnos, the Celtic
Horned God, the god of the hunt and of all wild things, bore the
antlers of a stag on his forehead. Several Scottish clans bear stags
or stags' heads on their coats of arms.

Wolf

The wolf has never enjoyed a happy relationship with humanity,
and is almost always portrayed as savage, rapacious and cruel. The
Pictish wolf could refer to a powerful warrior, strong and
ferocious, and unconcerned with any negative
connotations. Such a character might prefer
to frighten his enemies rather than choose a
more flattering representation. A much later

example of this attitude was the late 14th-century Alexander
Stewart, the 'Wolf of Badenoch', a wild, dangerous and bloody
man who cared nothing for public opinion, as long as people
feared him.

Animal Heads

There are occasional carved heads or head and necks of animals.
Some of them are recognisable, such as the Ardross Deer in
Inverness Museum; others are not, such as the dog-like
flippered creature portrayed on one of the stones at the entrance
to the graveyard at **Rhynie Old Church**. A
similar mystery animal head appears, along with a
double disc and z-rod, on two silver plaques
found at Norrie's Law in Fife – now in the

Museum of Scotland in Edinburgh. It has been
suggested that they represent masks or
headgear.

   Many other animals, both real and fantastic,
appear on Pictish stones. Some of the latter – for example the
centaur – do not belong to the usual run of Celtic mythology and
must have been imported, perhaps through the early bestiaries

whose religious allegories were often used to spread the Gospels. Other animal carvings, such as lions, bears and hyenas, probably have a similar origin.

WRITING

Some Pictish stones carry inscriptions in Latin or Ogham, an ancient Celtic alphabet. The Latin inscriptions are decipherable, but – even though the alphabet is easily understood (see next page) – most of the Ogham is not. This may be because the sculptor only carved a few letters of each word, in the same way as Roman inscriptions are abbreviated; after all, carving every letter into stone was laborious and time-consuming. Or the Ogham may have been carved in imitation, mimicking a skill no longer understood. One stone, at **Newton House** near Inverurie, carries Ogham lettering as well as a second inscription in an unrecognised alphabet. It has been suggested that this second inscription is merely imitation lettering, carved by an illiterate sculptor.

The profusion of carved stones is the source of the fascination – and the frustration – of the Picts. Their symbols do have meaning: they were once recognised and understood by a whole population. And if only the code could be cracked, their stories are still there to be read. Unfortunately, the information is not available to make anything other than guesses. Literally, your guess is as good as anyone else's. And who knows? Perhaps you will help to decode this ancient puzzle.

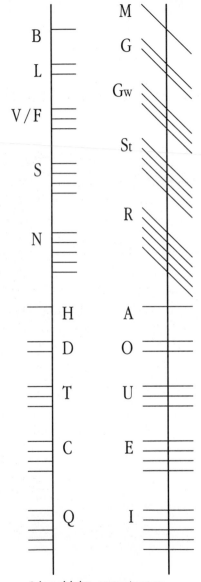

Ogham alphabet – see previous page.

34

Pictish sites and museums

Glamis Manse, Pictish symbol stone and cross-slab

Map of Pictish sites and museums

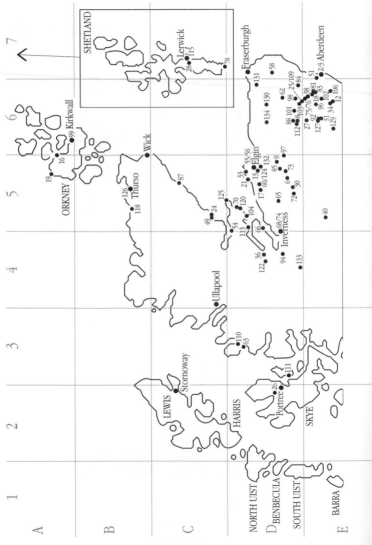

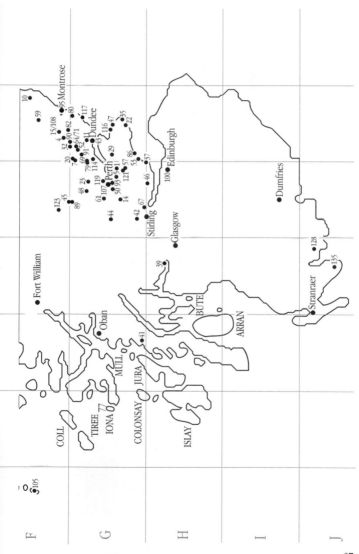

Key

P	Parking
S	Sales Area
R	Refreshments
W C	Toilet
£	Admission Charge

HS (Historic Scotland)
NTS (National Trust for Scotland)

Numbers before entries refer to the map on page 36-37.
All sites are normally closed 25/26 Dec. and 1/2 Jan.
Last entrance to properties can be well before closing.

*Rhynie Man – currently in the care of Aberdeenshire
Council.*

List of Pictish sites and museums

Although some of the Pictish stones and sites listed below are official historic monuments and open to the public, many are not, and are situated in private gardens or in fields belonging to working farms. Permission to view these stones should always be sought in advance, and one should never cross fields containing growing crops without express consent. If a site cannot be found using the main entry, try consulting the index.

1 Abdie Church (G5)
NO 259163 59
On minor road off B937, 3 miles SE of Newburgh, Fife
Originally located on the crest of the nearby Kaim Hill, this stone bears a cauldron above a fine crescent and v-rod. When it was moved to Abdie Church, a mirror symbol was found on one side. The stone, sometimes known as the Lindores Stone, also has a more recent sundial and OS benchmark carved into it.
NOTE: Access at all reasonable times

2 Aberdeen Marischal Museum (E7)
Marischal College, Broad Street, Aberdeen
The museum holds several Pictish stones and artifacts from across Scotland, including the Goose, Collace and Fairy Green stones – tel to confirm if on display.
NOTE: [Tel: 01224 274301] Open all year: Mon-Fri 10.00-17.00, Sun 14.00-17.00 (Web: www.abdn.ac.uk/diss/historic/)

P nearby S WC

3 Aberdeenshire Council Offices (E7)
Woodhill House, Westburn Road, Aberdeen
The Council has a fine Class 1 stone found near Rhynie, known as Rhynie Man, a ferocious axe-wielding giant with sharpened teeth. The stone is not currently on display, and there is some discussion as to where it will be located.
NOTE: [Tel: 01224 664723] – tel to confirm viewing arrangements

4 Aberlemno (F6)
NO 523557 54 HS
Off B9134, 6 miles NE of Forfar, Angus
A renowned group of Pictish stones, the most impressive and elaborate of which is undoubtedly the double-sided cross-slab standing in Aberlemno churchyard. Over 2 metres high, the front of the stone carries a full-length cross in high relief, decorated

with intricate inter-laced designs and surrounded by fan-tastic intertwining animals. On the reverse, the whole scene is framed by two serpents whose open-jawed head meet at the apex of the stone. They surround an extra-ordinary depiction of a battle – one of the very few examples of Pictish sculpture for which a convincing explanation can be made. Situated boldly above the battle are two Pictish symbols – a notched rectangle and z-rod and a cauldron – and these must surely have a strong association with the events shown below. Under-

neath is almost a comic-strip depiction of a battle, reading left to right and top to bottom. In the first strip, the mounted warrior on the left is chasing away another horseman wearing a helmet with a prominent noseguard, whose sword, shield and spear lie abandoned behind him. The second strip shows three foot-soldiers confronting another mounted warrior wearing a similar helmet. The third and final strip shows two more horsemen fighting; again, the one on the right wears a helmet with a prominent noseguard. The final scene shows the outcome of this engagement; the helmeted warrior lies dead on the ground, his shield beside him, and a carrion bird pecks at his face. This has been convincingly interpreted as a depiction of the Battle of Nechtansmere, fought in 685, a few miles south of Aberlemno near the modern village of Dunnichen. The helmets, with the distinctive noseguards, are identical to the 8th century Anglian helmet discovered at the Coppergate excavation in York; this cross-slab undoubtedly illustrates the decisive defeat of the Northumbrian Angles which broke forever their power north of the Forth and marked the beginning of their decline.

A second double-sided cross-slab stands by the roadside in Aberlemno. Although badly weathered much of the original carving can still be clearly seen. The front shows a full-length ringed cross whose decorations echo the jewelled metal crosses of the time. The cross is flanked by two angels in attitudes of prayer or mourning, while two fantastic animals lie crouched at its base. The reverse of the slab carries two large and highly decorated Pictish symbols, a crescent and v-rod and a double-disc and z-rod, above a scene of mounted huntsmen with hounds and trumpeters. At the bottom there are two separate panels showing a centaur in one and David, with sheep and harp, killing a lion in the other.

Situated on the roadside, about a quarter of a mile north of the church, stands one of the finest examples of a Class 1 stone. Nearly 2 metres tall, its carvings are deeply incised and clearly visible, showing a serpent above a double-disc and z-rod and a mirror and comb. There are cup-marks low down on one side, suggesting that this may be a prehistoric standing stone reused by the Picts.

NOTE: All stones enclosed for protection from 1 Oct-31 Mar and cannot be viewed during that time

P nearby

5 Abernethy (G5)

NO 190165 58 HS
On A913, 6 miles SE of Perth, Perth & Kinross

The imposing round tower, all that remains of an important and ancient monastic centre, is one of only two such Irish-style towers remaining in Scotland — the other is in Brechin. The ruins of an iron-age fort, possibly still in use during the Pictish period, stands on top of the hill overlooking the town. A Class 1 stone, discovered in the early 19th century, is now located at the base of the tower. It shows a vertical tuning fork, prongs pointing downward, between a hammer and anvil (possible axe-head?), above the remains of a crescent and v-rod. Four other symbol stones from Abernethy are in the **Museum of Scotland**, Edinburgh. There is a museum in Abernethy.

NOTE: Stone: access at all reasonable times; tower: open Apr-Sep: key available locally

P nearby

6 Advie Church (D5)

NJ 127343   28

Set into north wall of church in Advie, on minor road off A95, 9 miles NE of Grantown-on-Spey, Highland

This fragment was found in the burial ground in 1906, and shows part of a crescent and v-rod and disc and rectangle. It is built into the north wall of the church.

NOTE: Access at all reasonable times

P nearby

7 Alyth (G6)

NO 243488   53

Off B954, in porch of Alyth High Kirk, Alyth, Perthshire

Found in the late 19th century, this Class 2 cross-slab shows a decorated cross set near the top of the front of the stone, with four spirals in the background. The reverse of the slab shows part of a double disc and z-rod.

NOTE: Access at all reasonable times

P nearby

8 Ardlair (D6)

NJ 555287   37

Beside B9002 , 4 miles E of Rhynie, Aberdeenshire

This stone was noticed next to a nearby prehistoric stone circle, and may have been reused by the Picts. It carries a Pictish beast next to a tuning fork above a mirror.

NOTE: On private property – permission should be sought in advance

9 Arndilly House (D5)

NJ 291471   28

Set in a wall near Arndilly House, 1.5 miles N of Dandalieth on minor road off A95, Moray

This Class 1 stone shows a disc and rectangle beside a notched rectangle and z-rod.

NOTE: On private property – permission should be sought in advance

10 Auquhollie Farmhouse (F6)

NO 823907   45

In field beside minor road off A957, 5 miles NW of Stonehaven, Kincardine & Deeside

This stone, some 2.5 metres tall, bears an Ogham inscription which reads VUONON TEDOV.

11 Balluderon (St Martin's Stone) (G6)

NO 375376 54

In field west of A929, 5 miles N of Dundee, Angus

This broken cross-slab, known as Martin's or St Martin's Stone, stands 1.2 metres tall. On the front can be seen part of a mounted man in the bottom of the cross-shaft. On the back is a Pictish beast beside a horseman, all above a snake and z-rod.

NOTE: On private property – permission should be sought in advance

Stone with z-rod carving, held at the the Museum of Scotland.

12 Banchory House (E6)

NJ 915024 38

In walled garden at Banchory House, on minor road off B9077, 2 miles SE of Aberdeen

Six Class 1 stones were found on top of a rock-stack in Strathlethan Bay, near Stonehaven. Five of the stones are on display here: one shows a salmon below a small triangle; the second, a crescent and another triangle; the third, two adjacent discs – perhaps a double-disc; the fourth, a double-disc and z-rod. The fifth stone is a rough cuboid, and has various unusual letter-like designs carved on its four vertical surfaces. The sixth stone, showing a double-disc and z-rod beside a flower, mirror and comb, is housed in the **Aberdeen Marischal Museum**.

NOTE: On private property – permission should be sought in advance

13 Birnie Kirk (D5)

NJ 206587 28

Off B9010, 2.5 miles S of Elgin, Moray

A Class 1 boulder, with an eagle and a notched rectangle and z-rod, stands outside the church. The church itself, standing on a kirkyard mound and dedicated to St Brendan, dates back to the 12th century, and was once the seat of the Bishops of Moray.

NOTE: Stone and church: access at all reasonable times

P

14 Blackford (G5)

NN 924098   58
Peterhead Farm, on minor road off A9, 3 miles S of Auchterarder, Perthshire
A Class 1 stone incised with a rectangle and a bird. Some see it as a goose, but others – because of its proximity to Gleneagles – interpret it as an eagle.

15 Brechin Cathedral (F6)

NO 596601   44
Off A935, Brechin, Angus

Originally found in the chapel of Aldbar Castle, this Class 3 cross-slab is now located in Brechin Cathedral, which itself dates back to the 12th century. Beside the cathedral stands an Irish-style round tower, similar to the tower in Abernethy, which dates from the 11th century. The front of the cross-slab shows a ringed cross, decorated with an interlaced design, standing on top of a curious key-patterned hollow square. The cross is flanked by two figures holding books – probably monks – and there are two very weathered birds in the top left and right corners. On the back of the slab are four more indistinct figures. Two more monks stand above a rendition of David in the conventional pose, rending a lion's jaws, and accompanied by a sheep and a harp. Beneath this David rides a mounted warrior; and below again stands a curious many-legged beast.

NOTE: Open all year [Tel: 01356 629360]

P nearby   S

16 Broch of Gurness (A5)

HY 381268   6   HS

Off A966, 14 miles NW of Kirkwall, Orkney

Defended by a series of ramparts, the site consists of the fine ruins of a broch and surrounding settlement. The settlement was occupied by the Picts, and artifacts found here include a stone carved with Pictish symbols. Remains of Pictish house. Museum with some Pictish artifacts. Involves walk.

NOTE: [Tel: 01856 751414] Open Apr-Sep, daily

P nearby S £

17 Brodie Castle (D5)

NH 980577   27   NTS

On minor road N of A96, 3.5 miles W of Forres, Moray

This 2-metre-high Class 2 cross-slab was found in the graveyard of the old church of Dyke and Moy, and stands now on the side of the avenue leading to Brodie Castle. The front of the stone shows a full-length cross, decorated with complex knotwork patterns. In the background are several pairs of interlocking animals, although much of the carving has been defaced. The back of the stone carries a pair of sea-monsters, flanking some unusual circular objects. Below is a Pictish beast and a double disc and z-rod. The stone has Ogham lettering carved all around it, but only a small part on the lower right-hand side can be read, spelling out what may be a personal name: EDDARRNON Q. A

cast of the stone is on display in **Inverness Museum and Art Gallery**.

NOTE: [Tel: 01309 641371] Grounds open all year, daily 9.30-sunset; castle open Apr-Oct – tel to confirm days and times

P   S   R   £   WC   Disabled limited access/WC

18 Broomend of Crichie (E6)

NJ 776197   38

Beside minor road off A96, 2 miles NW of Kintore, Aberdeenshire

This carved stone originally stood near a stone circle on Crichie Farm, but was re-erected between two other plain standing stones, all that remains of a prehistoric circle. The stone carries a Pictish beast carved above a crescent and v-rod.

19 Brough of Birsay (A5)

HY 239285   6   HS

Off A965 or A986, 20 miles NW of Kirkwall, Orkney

Site of Pictish settlement. A fine broken Pictish incised stone was found on the tidal island, the original of which is now kept at the **Museum of Scotland** in Edinburgh. A replica stands on the island, and there is a Pictish well. The remains of an early Christian and Norse settlement survive, including a 12th-century church.

NOTE: [Tel: 01856 841815] Tidal causeway to island: check tides

20 Bruceton (G6)

NO 290504   53

Off B954, in field 3.5 miles NE of Alyth, Perthshire

The location of this stone may be significant: it stands very near to the river Isla, the ancient boundary between Perthshire and Angus. It carries an arch above a Pictish beast, and stone coffins were excavated from near here.

NOTE: On private property – permission should be sought in advance

21 Burghead (D5)

NJ 110690   28

On minor road off B9089, 8 miles NW of Elgin, Moray

Burghead was an important iron-age seaport, and is the largest early historic fortress in Scotland. The massive ramparts and ditches which dominated the end of the promontory were clearly visible into the 19th century, but sadly most of them were destroyed during the remodelling of the town between 1805 and 1809. Radiocarbon dating suggests that the fort was built between the 4th and 6th centuries AD, and destroyed sometime in the 9th or 10th.

Many fine Pictish carvings were found here, including several incised bulls, which can now be seen on display through a window in Burghead Library, **Elgin Museum**, the **Museum of Scotland** in Edinburgh and the British Museum in London.

A fascinating underground well, dating from the Pictish period, still remains. Reached by a flight of worn steps, the well consists of a square rock-cut chamber containing a 1.3 metre deep tank surrounded by a platform, with a basin and pedestal in opposite corners. The well may have had a religious function, connected to an early Christian monastery nearby. It may also have had pagan associations: wells were often part of Celtic rituals, and perhaps involving sacrifice. There are even records of execution by drowning amongst the Picts. Remnants of ancient religious belief still survive; every January, the people of Burghead celebrate the burning of the Clavie – an echo of a pagan fire-festival – where a tar-filled barrel is set alight and carried around the village before being set up on the ramparts of the fort.

NOTE: Well – [Tel: 01667 460232] Access at all reasonable times; visitor centre with displays on Burghead [Tel: 01343 835518] Open Apr-Sep PM (www.burghead.com)

22 Caiplie Chapel Cave (G6)

NO 600058 59

S of A917, on coast between Anstruther and Crail, Fife

A z-rod can be seen carved into the wall of this cave, with several crosses superimposed on top.

23 Cargill (G5)

NO 148362 53

In rockery of Balholmie House, Cargill, off A93, Perthshire

This stone carries a curious spade-like carving of a rectangle with a vertical line beside another, larger, rectangle.

NOTE: On private property – permission should be sought in advance

24 Carn Liath Broch & Settlement (C5)

NC 870013 17 HS

On A9, 3 miles E of Golspie, Sutherland

Fine remains of a broch with its surrounding settlement. A silver brooch was found here, dating from the 4th or 5th century, suggesting the settlement was used by the Picts. The brooch is now held at the **Museum of Scotland** in Edinburgh.

NOTE: Access at all reasonable times – walk to site

P

25 Chapel of Garioch (Maiden Stone) (D6)

NJ 704247 38

On hillside next to minor road off A96, 1 mile NW of Chapel of Garioch, 5 miles NW of Inverurie, Aberdeenshire

Known as the Maiden Stone, this was a highly decorated Class 2 cross-slab, although much of the carving has been lost or defaced. At the head of the front of the stone, a man stands with arms outstretched, holding a sea-monster in each hand. Below this group is a ringed cross, with traces of interlaced decoration on either side. At the foot of the cross is what must once have been a large and intricately patterned disc, with triangular knots filling out the exterior corners. The back of the stone is less weathered and shows several beasts of various descriptions in the top panel; below is a large notched rectangle and z-rod; below that is a fine Pictish beast; and at the bottom is a mirror and double-sided comb.

Legend has it that a daughter of the Laird of Balquhain made a bet with the Devil that she could bake a supply of bread before he could build a road to the summit of Bennachie (the road is known as the Maiden Causeway, and runs from the fort on the summit (NJ 683224) to another at Maiden Castle (NJ 694244)). The Devil won the bet, but the woman fled and was transformed into this stone, whereby it gets its name. Of course, it could have been called the Maiden Stone for centuries, and attracted the tale by way of explanation.

NOTE: Access at all reasonable times

26 Clach Ard (D2)

NG 421491   23
Within railings off B8036, near Tote, Skye
A Class 1 stone with a crescent and v-rod, double disc and z-rod, and mirror and comb.
NOTE: Access at all reasonable times

27 Clatt (E6)

NJ 544241   37
Next to Knockespoke House, on minor road between A944 and B9002, 1.5 miles S of Clatt, Aberdeenshire
A Class 1 stone showing a cauldron above a double disc and a fragment of a mirror.
NOTE: On private property – permission should be sought in advance

Clach Ard – Pictish symbol stone

28 Clickhimin (C7)

HU 464408   4   HS
Off A970, 1 mile SW of Lerwick, Shetland
The ruins of a fine broch and settlement, which was probably used by the Picts.
NOTE: [Tel: 01856 841815] Access at all reasonable times

29 Collessie (G6)

NO 293133 59

In field by minor road off
B937, 0.25 miles E of Collessie,
Fife

This stone, nearly 3 metres tall,
carries an incised figure of a
naked warrior. Armed with a
large rectangular shield and a
long spear with a leaf-shaped
blade, he marches from right to
left across the top third of the
monolith. Two other faint
symbols, tentatively identified
as an arch and a Pictish beast,
have been found on the left-
hand edge, level with the
warrior's chest. Aerial photo-
graphs of the field have
identified traces of a series of
barrow-mounds. The stone fell

Collessie carved stone

over in 1984, but has since been re-erected and fixed into place.

NOTE: On private property – permission should be sought in advance

30 Congash (D5)

NJ 058262 36

On Congash Farm, beside A95 2 miles E of Speybridge, Highland

These two stones form the gateposts to the *Parc an Caipel* 'Field of the Chapel' –
a field which was once a churchyard. Both stones have sunk into the ground, and
only the upper halves are visible. One carries a Pictish beast below an arch; the
other bears a double disc and z-rod over a unique 'bow and arrow' symbol.

NOTE: On private property – permission should be sought in advance

31 Corrachree (E6)

NJ 462047 37

Behind Corrachree House, on minor road off A97 2 miles NW of Tarland,
Kincardine & Deeside

This Class 1 stone shows three circles in a disc above two obscured symbols.

NOTE: On private property – permission should be sought in advance

32 Cossans (St Orland's Stone) (F6)

NO 401500 54 HS

Beside minor road off A928, 3 miles S of Kirriemuir, Angus

Known as St Orland's Stone, this Class 2 cross-slab probably marks the position of an early Christian site. The front carries a full-length ringed cross, decorated with ornate interlaced patterns. The back of the stone is framed by two fish-tailed serpents holding something between their jaws – perhaps a human head, as at **Dunfallandy**. It shows a crescent and v-rod and a double disc and z-rod above four horsemen accompanied by hounds. Below these huntsmen is a boat with a large object in the stern, variously interpreted as a cargo or Christ and the evangelists. At the very bottom, an unidentified beast attacks a bull.

NOTE: Access at all reasonable times

33 Covesea Caves (D5)

NJ 175707 28
On coast N of B9040, between Lossiemouth Lighthouse and Hopeman, Moray

Carved stone, held at the Museum of Scotland.

Also known as the Sculptor's Cave, these large dry caves contain a variety of Pictish symbols incised into their walls. There may have been a connection to the major Pictish fort at **Burghead**.

NOTE: Access at all reasonable times – care should be taken

34 Craigmyle (E6)

NJ 640024 37
Off A980, on SW slope of Hill of Fare, 2 miles N of Banchory, Kincardine & Deeside
This Class 1 stone, 2.3 metres tall, carries a faint notched rectangle and z-rod above a snake.

NOTE: Access at all reasonable times

35 Crail Parish Church (G6)

NO 614080 59

On A917, Marketgate, Crail, Fife

This very worn Class 3 cross-slab, nearly 2 metres tall, now stands inside the south entrance to the church. It shows a man holding a tall cross; to the right is a seated figure, perhaps representing the enthroned Christ, or perhaps the Virgin and Child; with another figure standing behind. To the left, a bird pecks at various unidentified creatures. A coat-of-arms has been added at a later date to the bottom of the shaft. The church, dating from the 13th century, is a fine building.

NOTE: Open Jun-mid Sep

P nearby S WC Disabled access

36 Dingwall (D4)

NH 549589 26

Off A826 at south entrance to St Clement's churchyard, Dingwall, Ross

Probably a prehistoric monolith reused by the Picts, this stone has a double disc and z-rod with two crescents and v-rods on one side; on the other, there are three discs above a crescent and v-rod and a collection of much older cup-and-ring marks.

NOTE: Access at all reasonable times

37 Dogton (G5)

NT 236968 58 HS

On minor road off A92, in field at Dogton farm, 5 miles NW of Kirkcaldy, Fife

In poor condition, this cross stands within railings next to a wall by Dogton Farm. Identifiable carvings include a horseman with a spear, two interlaced serpents biting each other, and faint traces of an arch and Pictish beast.

NOTE: Access at all reasonable times – walk to site (not signposted)

38 Drimmies Farm (E6)

NJ 743235 38

Drimmies Farm, off A96 3 miles NW of Inverurie, Aberdeenshire

Now part of the wall of the entrance to Drimmies Farm, this Class 1 stone shows a mirror and double-sided comb with an s-shaped symbol.

NOTE: On private property – permission should be sought in advance

39 Dumbarton (H4)

NS 400745 64 HS

Off A814, Dumbarton

Standing on a massive rock on the north bank of the Clyde, Dumbarton was the stronghold of the Britons of Strathclyde. In 756 it was captured by the Picts and Northumbrians, and it was also taken in 870. Strathclyde was absorbed into the kingdom of Scots after the death of its last king, Owen the Bald, in 1018. The old stronghold was reused as a medieval castle, and the future David II (Robert the Bruce's son) and the infant Mary, Queen of Scots, were both kept safe here. The castle was developed in later centuries for artillery, obliterating most of the early work, and was garrisoned until World War II.

NOTE: [Tel: 01389 732167] Open all year, daily; closed Thu/Fri Oct-Mar

P S £ WC

40 Dunachton (E5)

NH 821046 35

Off A9, 5 miles NE of Kingussie, Highland

There is a Class 1 stone, showing an animal head, beside a garden wall at this location.

NOTE: On private property – permission should be sought in advance

41 Dunadd (G3)

NR 836936 55 HS

By minor road off A816, 3.5 miles S of Kilmartin, Argyll

Dating from the 1st century AD, the hill-fort of Dunadd rises dramatically from the flat flood-plain of the river Add. The climb to the top is steep, but well worth the effort. From their first arrival in Scotland, Dunadd was a stronghold of the Dalriadan Scots and the site of the inauguration of their kings – the Stone of Destiny was said to have been kept here. At the very summit of the hill is a rock with a basin, a footprint and a boar carved into it, probably used as part of the king-making ritual. Twice besieged by the Picts, in 683 and 736, Dunadd was of great importance, and some of the massive fortifications can still easily be seen today.

NOTE: Open all year – involves a steep and possibly slippy climb

42 Dunblane Cathedral (G5)

Off B8033, in Dunblane, Stirlingshire

Dunblane has been a Christian site since Pictish times, although most of the present cathedral dates from the 13th century. During restoration work in the late 19th century two carved stones were discovered which can now be seen in the cathedral. The first, and most impressive, is a ringed cross-slab, the front of which shows a cross, outlined with stone beading which terminates at the base in two serpent heads. On the back are several carvings: at the top, two animals face each other, standing on their hind legs with their forepaws crossed, beside a spiral carved in the upper right corner; under them is a square design with five round bosses; beneath that is a small ringed cross on the left, and an unidentified shape to the right; below these is a mounted hunter, armed with a spear and followed by a dog; underneath them is a disc and cross surrounded with spirals and other patterns; and at the very bottom is a man with a staff, lying with his feet towards the bottom right-hand corner where there is a second spiral, similar to that on the top right. The second stone shows various carved patterns and interlaced stylised animals.

NOTE: [Tel: 01786 825388] – Open all year, daily (from 13.30 Sun) (www.dunblanecathedral.org.uk)

P nearby S WC Disabled access

43 Dundee Museum (McManus Galleries) (G6)

McManus Galleries, Albert Square, Dundee

Dundee Museum tells the story of this historic region of Scotland from the earliest times to the present day. Carved stones form part of its permanent collection, supplemented by other excellent exhibits and information on the Picts, including the Dunnichen Stone found near the site of the Battle of Nechtansmere.

NOTE: [Tel: 01382 432250] Open all year, Mon-Sat 10.30-17.00, Sun 12.30-16.00

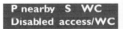

P nearby S WC
Disabled access/WC

44 Dundurn (G5)

NN 708233 52

Off A9 or A924, 4 miles W of Comrie, Perthshire

The hill fort, consisting of a citadel with a series of lower fortified terraces, was a major stronghold of the Picts. It was besieged in 683. Giric, one of the early kings of Scots, was slain at Dundurn in 889.

Dunfallandy symbol stone and cross-slab

45 Dunfallandy (F5)

NN 946564 53 HS

On minor road south of A9, 1 mile S of Pitlochry, Perthshire

This intriguing Class 2 cross-slab was moved in the late 19th century from the old chapel at Killiecrankie to its present location outside Dunfallandy House. The front shows a full-length cross, beautifully carved and decorated with spirals, knotwork and bosses, although the central panel is mysteriously blank. A whole menagerie of strange creatures surrounds the cross, including two four-winged angels and a sea-monster with a pair of human legs emerging from its jaws. The back is framed by two fish-tailed serpents, holding a human head between their jaws at the apex of the slab. The top third of the stone contains two seated figures facing each other over a small cross. The slightly smaller figure on the left has a Pictish beast above its head; the right-hand figure sits beneath a double disc and crescent and v-rod. The middle third shows a mounted figure riding from left to right, with another crescent and v-rod and Pictish beast in front. The bottom third shows a hammer, an anvil and a set of tongs. Does this represent a marriage of two families, with the offspring below inheriting one of each of the parents symbols? Do the blacksmith's tools represent the profession, or are they an allegory for the forging of new bonds?

NOTE: Open all year (not signposted) – enclosed in protective glass case

46 Dunfermline Abbey (H5)

NT 088874 65 HS

Off A9, in Dunfermline, Fife

The Picts had an important centre here. Queen Margaret, wife of Malcolm Canmore, founded an abbey at Dunfermline in the 11th century, the church and ruins of which survive. Many of the kings of queens of Scots were buried here, and the body of Robert the Bruce is buried in the church (choir of church closed Oct-Apr).

NOTE: [Tel: 01383 739026] Open all year except Thu PM & Fri Oct-Mar

P nearby S £

47 Dunino Den (G6)

NO 541109 59

On B9131, in Dunino, 4 miles SE of St Andrews, Fife

Steps cut into the rock lead down from the church to a large hollow, shaped by the action of the burn which runs through it. A bowl and footprint have been carved out of the stone above the water; perhaps, as at **Dunadd** in Argyll which has a similar basin and footprint, kings were once inaugurated here. A huge ringed cross, nearly 3 metres tall and 2 metres wide, has been cut into the cliff-face overlooking the hollow. In the churchyard above stands a very weathered cross-slab with crosses crudely incised into both sides.

NOTE: Open all year – access is by worn stone steps: care needed

Carved stone, held at the Museum of Scotland.

48 Dunkeld Cathedral (G5)

NO 025426   53   HS

Off A923, in Dunkeld, Perthshire

Dunkeld was a royal site in Pictish times, and played an important role in the unification of the Pictish and Scottish kingdoms. The Cathedral, whose 14th-century choir is still used as the parish Church, houses a large Class 3 stone. The front is quite badly weathered, but the remains of a cross and several scenes can still be made out, the most obvious being a man, kneeling in prayer, surrounded by four animals – probably Daniel in the lions' den. On the back, there are three panels which show: a group of about 16 heads and a circular disc, interpreted either as the Israelites crossing the Red Sea or the Feeding of the Five Thousand; the two panels below show six figures each and probably represent the Twelve Apostles. The Cathedral tower also houses a fragment of another stone, showing a mounted man with a horn and a spear.

NOTE: Open all year, 10.00-16.00 (www.dunkeldcathedral.org.uk)

P nearby   S   WC   Disabled access

49 Dunrobin Museum (C5)

NC 852008   17

On minor road off A9, 1.5 miles E of Golspie, Sutherland

Set in the grounds of Dunrobin Castle, the seat of the Earls of Sutherland since the 13th century and well worth a visit in itself, Dunrobin Museum holds an excellent collection of Pictish stones from around the area, both whole and fragmentary, including a cross-slab (Golspie Stone) from St Andrews kirkyard with Pictish symbols and an Ogham inscription. (www.highlandescape.com/index.html)

NOTE: [Tel: 01408 633177] Open Apr-mid Oct; opening times vary

P   S   R   WC   £   Disabled access/WC

50 Dupplin Cross (St Serf's Church, Dunning) (G5)

NO 019145   58

In St Serf's Church, Dunning, on B8052, 5 miles E of Auchterarder, Perthshire

The Dupplin Cross, formerly standing near to the site of the ancient royal palace at Forteviot, is a free-standing cross some 2.7 metres tall and beautifully carved all over. Carved in the 9th or 10th century, the Cross carries no mysterious symbols: only interlace, knotwork, scrolled designs, animals, biblical scenes and warriors, although the quality of the carving surely comes from Pictish hands. One panel even contains a Latin inscription, recently identified as CU[...]NTIN FILIUS FIRCUS – Constantine Mac Fergus, a Pictish King (c. 789–820) who ruled jointly over both Picts and Scots. The Dupplin Cross dates comes from the very end of the Pictish period, and symbolises the beginnings of the new, unified kingdom of Scots. The cross is now housed in the tower of the historic St Serf's Church in Dunning.

NOTE: Key available locally

P

51 Dyce (E7)

NJ 875154 38 HS

At Dyce Church, by minor road off A947, 1.5 miles NW of Dyce, Aberdeenshire

There are two carved stones here. The first, a Class 1 stone showing a Pictish beast above a double disc and z-rod, is built into the east wall of the church. The second is a Class 2 cross-slab, with a decorated cross on the front. On the back is a crescent and v-rod over a cauldron, and a disc and rectangle, containing concentric circles, above a double disc and z-rod. Removed for conservation (Tel: 01667 460232).

P

52 Eassie (G6)

NO 353474 54 HS

On minor road off A94, 6 miles SW of Kirriemuir, in Eassie Church, Angus

Standing in the ruins of Eassie Church, this very early Class 2 cross-slab displays a full-length cross decorated with intricate interlaced designs. Above either arm of the cross stands a four-winged angel (the top right is damaged). Below the left arm is a bearded huntsman carrying a spear and square shield, his cloak streaming behind him as he strides from left to right. Opposite to him is his quarry, a fine antlered stag, above an unidentified beast with its tail between its legs, above another animal, perhaps a hunting-dog. On the back of the stone is a Pictish beast above a double disc and z-

rod; three robed proc-essional figures; a man with a rod over his shoulder next to a fruit-tree: perhaps Adam and the Tree of Life, or a character from Celtic mythology; and a badly eroded scene with cattle and perhaps an arch. The stone has recently been cleaned, and is now encased in glass for protection.

NOTE: Access at all reasonable times

P nearby

53 East Wemyss Caves (G6)

NT 344972   59

Off the A955, East Wemyss, Fife

There are five caves at the shore-line of East Wemyss, four of which contain incised Pictish symbols, including double discs, crescents and v-rods, a mirror and animal heads, as well as a figure with a spear and a boat with oars. The caves are open to the public but access is not always easy.

NOTE: Caves open all year – care should be taken

54 Edderton (D5)

NH 708851   21

On minor road off A836, 5 miles NW of Tain, Ross

This massive prehistoric monolith stands over 3 metres high, and is clearly associated with a nearby stone circle. The Picts later carved into it a salmon and double disc and z-rod.

55 Elgin Cathedral (D5)

NJ 222632   28   HS

Off A96, Elgin, Moray

Known as the 'Lantern of the North', Elgin Cathedral dates from the 13th century, and now houses a Class 2 cross-slab within its substantial ruins. The cross-slab is over 2 metres high and shows a decorated cross with two winged figures, one over each arm. Below the left arm is one of the four Evangelists, St Matthew, with his symbol of a Man above him; below the right arm is another Evangelist, St John, beneath his eagle symbol. Beneath the cross are four intertwined beasts. The back of the stone shows a double disc and z-rod, a crescent and v-rod, and four mounted huntsmen with hounds in pursuit of a stag. One huntsman carries a hawk, and a game-bird sits on the ground in front of him.

NOTE: [Tel: 01343 547171] Open all year, except Thu and Fri Oct-Mar

P nearby   S   £
Disabled access

56 Elgin Museum (D5)

High Street, Elgin
This award-winning museum holds many items of interest relating to both the prehistory and history of the North-East, including some of the **Burghead** stones and others from Kinneddar. Museum refurbishment is under way: due to reopen August.
NOTE: [Tel: 01343 543675] Open Apr-Oct, tel to confirm
(www.elginmuseum.org.uk)

P nearby S WC
£ Disabled
limited access/
W C

Carved stone, Edderton – see previous page.

57 Falkland Palace (G5)

Just north of A912, in Falkland, Fife
Falkland Palace, well worth visiting for its own sake, has two Pictish Class 1 stones, found at the nearby Westfield Farm in 1971, on display in the museum. The first stone shows two arches, one above the other, and a notched rectangle; the second shows a single disc and rectangle next to a fragment of a double disc.
NOTE: [Tel: 01337 857397] Open Mar-Oct, Mon-Sat 10.00-18.00, Sun 13.00-17.00

P S R WC £

58 Fetterangus (D7)

NJ 981506 30
On minor road between A950 and A952, 2.5 miles N of Old Deer, Buchan
This Class 1 stone is fixed to the wall on the right-hand side of the entrance to the old churchyard. It shows a scrolled curving line above a disc and rectangle, with a cauldron beneath. The symbols may be hard to discern in most light conditions, and are very weathered.
NOTE: Access at all reasonable times

59 Fordoun Church (St Palladius Stone) (F6)

NO 726784   45

On minor road off A90, 10 miles SW of Stonehaven, Kincardine & Deeside

Standing in the porch of Fordoun Church, this Class 2 cross-slab is unusual in that it bears writing: in the top left-hand corner, the name PIDARNOIN is spelled out. It was found in the old Fordoun Church when that building was being demolished. The stone is broken at the top, and shows a cross with decorations and carvings in the arms: the top arm shows a piece of a sea-monster; the left arm – and probably the right – has knotwork decoration; and the lower arm contains a warrior on horseback holding a spear. He is flanked by two more horsemen, accompanied by a hound and another creature. Beneath is a double disc and z-rod.

NOTE: Access at all reasonable times

60 Forres (Falconer) Museum (D5)

Off B9010, in Forres, Moray

The museum houses exhibits covering the history and heritage of Moray from prehistory to the present, including information on the Picts.

NOTE: [Tel: 01309 673701] Open all year, opening times vary

P S WC   Disabled limited access/WC

61 Fowlis Wester (G5)

NN 928240   52   HS

On minor road off A85, 5 miles E of Crieff, Perthshire

This Class 2 cross-slab, known as the Cross of Fowlis, over 3 metres tall, now stands inside Fowlis Wester Parish Church, with an excellent replica on the original site in the village. The front shows a tall cross, with carved decoration inside the arms. There are faint traces of animals and birds at the base. On the back are several horsemen, probably in a hunt as one carries a hawk, riding across the stone beneath a double disc. There is also a strange procession, headed by a man in a long robe, leading a cow with a bell round its neck, followed by six figures. A crescent and v-rod sits next to a bird, possibly an eagle, and at the very bottom a monster is

59

devouring a man. The iron chain attached to the stone is probably the remains of a jougs, an iron collar to which petty criminals would be attached for public ridicule, a practice which continued from medieval times to the 18th and possibly early 19th century.

The church holds a second carved stone. It is set tight up against a wall and no-one knows what is carved on the back, and at present is classified as Class 3. It is dominated by a large ringed cross, filled with interlaced decoration, sitting on a square base. Top left and right show Jonah being swallowed by the whale, and then disgorged again – the Old Testament story of Jonah was seen as a parallel to the death and resurrection of Christ. On the left side of the cross is St Paul, seated on a throne, beside representations of the date-palms that fed him in the wilderness. On the right, a seated St Anthony is visited by an angel. Two monks stand below St Paul, but the carving below St Anthony has been obscured.

NOTE: Open daily

62 Fyvie (D6)

NJ 769378   29

On minor road off B9005, 10 miles NW of Old Meldrum, Buchan

There are three carved stones here, which have been built into the exterior wall of the church. Two are definitely Pictish Class 1 stones: one shows part of a crescent and v-rod, a Pictish beast and a mirror; the other bears part of an eagle and a double disc. The latter has been placed above the third, a granite stone 1.5 metres high, which has been carved with interlaced designs and circles. Also a stone found at Rothiebrisbane decorated with three circles in a disc.

NOTE: Access at all reasonable times

63 Gairloch Heritage Museum (D3)

On A832, in Gairloch, Ross

The museum has displays covering all aspects of life in the Western Highlands, from prehistory to the present day, including information on the Picts and a carved stone with a salmon and part of an eagle. (www.GairlochHeritageMuseum.org.uk)

NOTE: [Tel: 01445 712287] Open Easter-Oct, times vary, and by appt

P S R WC £ Disabled access/WC

64 Glamis Manse (G6)

NO 386469   54

Opposite church, on minor road off A94, in Glamis, Angus

This intriguing Class 2 cross-slab may have connections with the nearby healing well of St Fergus, as many of its motifs can be interpreted as relating to healing. The front of the cross is dominated by a beautifully carved full-length cross, decorated with intricately interlaced designs. In the top left-hand corner is an unusual animal with clawed feet and a long tail curled over its back, possibly representing the lion of St Mark. In the top right is a remarkable centaur, holding an axe in each hand. This has been interpreted as representing Chiron, who cut the branch of healing and gave it to Asklepios, the Greek god of medicine. Bottom left shows two warriors, armed with axes and locked in combat. Above them is a cauldron – realistically depicted, side on – with two pairs of human legs protruding from it. This perhaps is the Cauldron of Dagda, capable of curing battle wounds and even resurrecting the slain. In the bottom right is an animal's head – perhaps a lamb, representing Christ – over a large cauldron symbol. The back of the stone bears a salmon, a snake and a mirror. The nearby church, dedicated to St Fergus, is also open to the public, and the well can also be visited via a landscaped trail.

The fine and interesting Glamis Castle, which is regularly open to the public, is located nearby, as is the Angus Folk Museum (NTS).

NOTE: Stone, well and church: access at all reasonable times

P nearby   S nearby

65 Glenferness House (Princess Stone) (D5)

NH 937426 27

Near Glenferness House, on minor road off B9007, 3 miles SW of Ferness, Highland

A very worn Class 2 cross-slab, known as the Princess Stone, standing some 300 metres from Glenferness House. The front of the stone bears a ringed cross, above two wrestlers, with spiral designs in the background. On the back, an archer kneels in front of a crescent and v-rod and a Pictish beast. Below the archer is a hound, a double disc and z-rod and another Pictish beast.

NOTE: On private property – permission should be sought in advance

66 Groam House Museum & Pictish Centre (D5)

On A832, 1 mile NE of Fortrose, on High Street, Rosemarkie, Ross

Rosemarkie was a major ecclesiastical centre in early Christian times. This award-winning museum holds 15 Class 2 and 3 stones, all found within the village, as testament to its importance. Pride of place goes to the Rosemarkie Cross, a beautiful and intricately decorated Class 2 stone which must be seen to be appreciated. The museum also boasts a fine collection of audio-visual and static displays, activities and temporary exhibitions – highly recommended.

NOTE: [Tel: 01381 620961] Open Easter week and May-Sep, Mon-Sat 10.00-17.00, Sun 14.00-16.30; Oct-Apr, Sat-Sun 14.00-16.00

P S WC £ Disabled limited access/WC

67 Hawkhill (G5)

NS 902926 58
By minor road off A907, 0.5 miles E of Alloa, Clackmannanshire
This 2.5 metre tall slab, incised front and back with long crosses, may have originally been a tombstone: an excavation in the early 19th century discovered many human bones around its base.

68 Highland Council Chambers (Knock-nagael Boar Stone) (D4)

Rosemarkie Cross, Groam House Museum.

Glenurquhart Road, Inverness HS
The Council Chambers houses the Knocknagael Boar Stone, moved in 1991 for conservation from Essich. The stone carries a beautiful incised carving of a boar beneath a disc and rectangle. It can be viewed through a window at all times.
NOTE: [Tel: 01463 702000] Open all year during Council hours

69 Hill of Keillor (G6)

NO 273397 53
By minor road off A923 on north slope of Hill of Keillor opposite entrance to High Keillor farm, 4 miles E of Coupar Angus, Perthshire
A Class 1 stone bearing a wolf-like creature and a double disc and z-rod is located on a small mound, which was found to contain cists and bones when excavated.

70 Hilton of Cadboll (D5)

NG 873768 21

Hilton of Cadboll, off B9165, 7 miles SE of Tain, Ross and Cromarty, Highland

The fine carved stone, which had been reused as a burial marker, is now in the **Museum of Scotland**, while a modern replacement has been placed at the site. There are also the grass-covered foundations of a chapel.

NOTE: Access at all reasonable times

P nearby

71 Hunter's Hill (G6)

NO 394465 54

In wood on N slope of Hunter's Hill, 0.25 miles SE of Glamis, Angus

Carved stone, Inveravon Church – see next page

This Class 2 cross-slab carries a tall cross on the front. In the top right corner is a four-winged angel; top left is a bird-headed man carrying an axe, facing another figure, now largely obscured – perhaps similar to the figures at the base of the cross-slab from Papil, now in the **Museum of Scotland**. The lower left shows a group of deer; and lower right holds two creatures above a cauldron and a flower. The back bears an unidentified creature, a serpent and part of a mirror. It is in a small enclosure with railings.

NOTE: Access at all reasonable times

72 Inverallan (D5)

NJ 027269 36

Inverallan burial ground, on minor road off A95, 2 miles SW of Grantown-on-Spey, Highland

A Class 1 stone, bearing a crescent and v-rod and a notched rectangle and z-rod: the carving is now quite faint. The stone was found when the old church was demolished, and is located on the inner side of the burial ground wall on the western side. In the cemetery stands Figgat's Cross, an early Christian monument.

NOTE: Access at all reasonable times

73 Inveravon Church (D5)

NJ 183376   28

On minor road off A95, at St Peters, 1 mile NW of Bridge of Avon, Moray
Four Class 1 stones are displayed against the south wall of the church. The finest shows a disc and notched rectangle above an eagle and a mirror and comb. The other stones respectively bear: a crescent and v-rod, a cauldron and a mirror and comb; a crescent and v-rod and a Pictish beast; and the head of a Pictish beast.
NOTE: Access at all reasonable times

74 Inverness Museum & Art Gallery (D4)

Castle Wynd, Inverness
The Inverness Museum has an excellent collection of Pictish artifacts and displays, and several fine Class 1 stones including the beautiful Ardross Wolf and Deer. The Picts had a major stronghold here. The site was reused for a medieval castle, the last vestiges of which were removed after being blown up in the Jacobite Rising. The site of the old stronghold is now occupied by a mock castle of 1835.
NOTE: [Tel: 01463 237114] Open all year, Mon-Sat 9.00-17.00; closed Sun and Public Holidays in winter (www.invernessmuseum.com)

P   S   R   WC   Disabled access

75 Inverurie (Brandsbutt Stone) (E6)

NJ 760224   38

Off A96, Gordon Terrace, Brandsbutt, in Inverurie, Aberdeenshire
Known as the Brandsbutt Stone, this Class 1 stone bears a crescent and v-rod and a snake and z-rod. The stone had been smashed and built into a nearby dyke, and not all of it was found when reassembled, the missing pieces being replaced by cement. The stone also carries an Ogham inscription, reading IRATADDOARENS.
NOTE: Access at all reasonable times

76 Inverurie Old Church (E6)

NJ 780206   38

In Inverurie Old Churchyard, on B993, Inverurie, Aberdeenshire
There are four fragments here, which all bear Class 1 symbols, and are located some 40 metres left of the entrance.

The first carries a crescent and v-rod, a disc and rectangle, a double disc and z-rod and a snake and z-rod. The second shows parts of a disc and an arch. The third bears part of a disc and a double disc and z-rod.

The most striking is the fourth, which shows a horse, trotting from left to right. This is the only time a horse has been found without a rider, and some question whether it is a true Pictish carving.
NOTE: Access at all reasonable times

77 Iona (G2)

NM 287245 48 HS
Off A849, isle of Iona, on west side of Mull

The peaceful and picturesque island from where St Columba left to convert the Picts in the 6th century. Features of the island include the restored 13th-century abbey and 9th-century shrine of St Columba, the picturesque ruinous nunnery, as well as a magnificent collection of early Christian sculpture, including St Martin's and St John's Crosses, and later stone effigies and grave-slabs. Many of the early kings of Scots are buried here in *Reilig Odhrain* (Oran's Cemetery) by the 'Street of the Dead'.

Parking and ferry (&) at Fionnphort: no cars on Iona.

NOTE: [Tel: 01681 700512]
Open daily all year

P S R £ WC
Limited disabled access

Rosemarkie Cross, Groam House Museum – page 61.

78 Jarlshof (C7)

HU 398095 4 HS
Off A970, 22 miles S of Lerwick, Shetland

Site of a Pictish settlement, some of which survives. Artifacts, including a slate decorated with a Pictish cross, have been found here. The site was occupied for centuries, and remains survive of a bronze age settlement, iron age broch, and a Norse settlement.

NOTE: [Tel: 01950 460112] Open Apr-Sep, daily

P nearby S £ WC

79 Kettins (G5)

NO 238391 53
In Kettins churchyard, on minor road off A923 2 miles SE of Coupar Angus, Perthshire

This Class 3 cross-slab is very worn, and was once used as a footbridge over Kettins burn. It carries the remains of a cross and four blurred scenes: a creature with its tail curved over its back; a winged animal holding something in its jaws; a man in a cloak flanked by two others with animal heads; and two intertwined creatures biting each other's tails.

80 Kinblethmont House (G6)

NO 638473   54

On minor road off B965, Inverkeillor, 6 miles N of Arbroath, Angus

Standing in the grounds of Kinblethmont House, this Class 1 stone shows a crescent and v-rod, a Pictish beast and part of a mirror and comb.

NOTE: On private property – permission should be sought in advance

Kintore

81 Kinellar Church (E6)

NJ 821145   38

On minor road off A96, 6 miles SE of Inverurie, Aberdeenshire

Standing in the hallway of the church, this is a Class 1 stone bearing a crescent and v-rod beneath three discs in a circle. It was found in the foundations of the church.

NOTE: Open all year

82 Kinnell (F6)

NO 609504   54

On minor road off B965, 2 miles E of Friockheim, Angus

Built into the top of the manse wall, all that can be seen of the carving is two coiled snakes, side by side, facing away from each other.

83 Kintore (E6)

NJ 793163   38

Off A96, in Kintore churchyard, Aberdeenshire

Once reused as a gravestone, but since re-erected, this is a Class 1 stone with a crescent and v-rod and Pictish beast on one side, and a salmon and cauldron on the other.

NOTE: Access at all reasonable times.

84 Kirkton of Bourtie (D6)

NJ 805249 38

On minor road off A947, 2 miles S of Old Meldrum, Aberdeenshire

This broken Class 1 stone is built high up into the exterior wall of the south wall of the church. It shows a crescent and v-rod above a double disc, with a mirror and comb.

NOTE: Access at all reasonable times

85 Knockando Church (D5)

NJ 187429 28

On minor road off B9102, 5 miles N of Bridge of Avon, Moray

Two Class 1 stones have been built into the churchyard wall. The first has a wheel-like design with radiating spokes, carved above two crescents, only one of which is crossed by a v-rod. The second stone carries a mirror and a snake.

NOTE: Access at all reasonable times

86 Largo (G6)

NO 423035 59

Off A915, in Largo, Fife

This large, broken and badly worn Class 2 cross-slab is currently housed in the gateway of Largo Parish Church. On the front is a long cross with a rectangular base. On the right hand side are two intertwined sea-monsters. The back of the slab bears three mounted huntsmen accompanied by hounds beside a double disc and z-rod, all above a Pictish beast and a deer (possibly two).

NOTE: Access at all reasonable times

87 Latheron (C5)

ND 199334 11

Near junction of A9 and A99 in Latheron, 18 miles SW of Wick, Caithness

Built into the south wall of the farmhouse at Latheron, this Class 1 slab carries a crescent and v-rod. Part of a Class 2 cross-slab was found here in 1903, and is now held in the **Museum of Scotland**.

NOTE: On private property – permission should be sought in advance

88 Leith Hall (D6)

NJ 540298 37 NTS

On minor road off B9002, 7 miles S of Huntly, Aberdeenshire

This piece of a Class 1 stone is now kept in a shelter in the gardens of Leith Hall. It bears the very bottom of a fish above an arch, while another stone is decorated with a rectangle above a wolf and mirror and comb.

NOTE: [Tel: 01464 831216] Grounds and gardens open all year, 9.30am-sunset. House open Easter, then May-Sep, Fri-Tue 12.00-17.00

P R £ Disabled access (limited access to House)

89 Logierait (G5)

NN 968520   53

Off A827, in Logierait, 5 miles SE of Pitlochry, Perthshire

Situated in Logierait churchyard, this Class 3 cross-slab is broken off near the top. It carries a decorated cross on the front; on the back is part of a mounted warrior, holding a spear, above a snake coiled around a pillar or tree. There is a second stone in the church.

NOTE: Open all year: check locally

90 Meffan Institute (F6)

20 West High Street, Forfar, Angus

This art gallery and museum holds an extensive collection of Pictish carved stones, both whole and fragmentary, all from Kirriemuir, and is well worth a visit. There is an excellent computer guide to Pictish stones.

(www.angus.gov.uk)

NOTE: [Tel: 01307 461460] Open all year, Mon-Sat 10.00-17.00

P nearby   S   WC
Disabled limited
access/WC

91 Meigle Museum (G6)

On A94, Meigle, Angus   HS

Justifiably described as one of the most notable collections of Dark Age sculpture anywhere in Western Europe, a visit to Meigle Museum is a must. The stones on display – over 30 in all – were found at or near the old churchyard, and include the beautiful and remar-kable Daniel Stone, with a depiction of Daniel and the lions. This stone, which formerly stood by a mound outside the church to the right of the north entrance, is said commemorate the burial place

of Guinevere (Vanora), wife of Arthur, who was reputedly torn apart for adultery.
NOTE: [Tel: 01828 640612] Open Apr-Sep, daily and by appt.

P nearby   S   WC   £   Disabled access/WC

92 Migvie (E6)

NJ 437068   37

On minor road off A97, 7 miles NE of Ballater, Kincardine and Deeside

Standing in the graveyard of Migvie Church, this unusual Class 2 cross-slab carries a large cross made up entirely of interlaced knotwork, with strange coils and loops at various corners. Above the left arm of the cross is a double disc and z-rod. Above the right arm is a unique symbol: an arch crossed by a v-rod. Bottom left is a pair of shears, and bottom right is a mounted man. The back of the stone has a second mounted figure.

NOTE: Access at all reasonable times

93 Moncrieffe House (Boar Stone of Gask) (G5)

NO 136193   58

On minor road off A9, 6 miles SW of Perth, Perthshire

Also known as the Boar Stone of Gask, this Class 2 cross-slab was moved to Moncrieffe House from near Gask around the end of the 19th century. Although much of the stone is badly worn, enough can still be seen to realise that this must once have been a very fine stone indeed. Both sides of the stone bear long crosses, surrounded by activity. One side is too weathered to make out any detail, but on the other can be seen centaurs, a double-headed monster, a strange horned beast with bulging eyes and a creature swallowing a serpent. The stone gets its name from the two boars with bristling ridges down their backs to the right of the cross. Also present are two horsemen, a flower symbol, and a snake and z-rod.

NOTE: On private property – permission should be sought in advance

94 Moniack Castle (D4)

NH 552435   26

On minor road off A862, 2.5 miles SE of Beauly, Highland

Moved to the grounds of Moniack Castle in 1903, the stone bears a bird-headed man carrying a club. Prehistoric cup-marks are also present.

NOTE: On private property – permission should be sought in advance

95 Montrose Museum & Art Gallery (F6)

Panmure Place, Montrose, Angus

The museum has a small collections of Pictish stones, including the striking Samson Stone, illustrating scenes from the Bible story including Samson slaying the Philistines with the jaw-bone of an ass and Delilah cutting off his hair. (www.angus.gov.uk)

NOTE: [Tel: 01307 461460] Open all year, Mon-Sat 10.00-17.00

P   S   WC   Disabled limited access/WC

96 Monymusk Church (St Mary's) (E6)

NJ 685152 38

On minor road off B993, 4 miles W of Kemnay, Aberdeenshire

Standing in Monymusk Parish Church, this fine Class 2 cross-slab is carved on one side only. It carries an elaborately decorated cross standing on a small curved base, above a stepped rectangle and a cauldron. The Monymusk Reliquary, a silver casket containing relics of St Columba, carried by the victorious Scottish army at Bannockburn, was sometimes displayed here. It can now be seen in the **Museum of Scotland**, Edinburgh.

NOTE: [Tel: 01467 651470] Check by tel.

97 Mortlach Church (D5)

NJ 324392 28

On minor road off B9009, 1 mile SW of Dufftown, Moray

Known as the Mortlach Battle Stone, this Class 2 cross-slab stands in Mortlach churchyard and bears a cross filled with spiral decoration. Two sea-monsters face each other over the top, and a strange short-legged beast crouches beneath. The back of the stone carries an eagle, a snake and the head of a bull above a huntsman and hound. There is also a Class 1 stone built into the entrance to the church, showing a Pictish beast and a curved design.

NOTE: Access at all reasonable times; church open Easter-Oct

98 Mounie Castle (D6)

NJ 767286 38

On minor road off A920, 3 miles W of Old Meldrum, Aberdeenshire

A Class 1 stone, found at Daviot, bearing a crescent and v-rod, above a mirror and comb, and a second crescent, this time without a rod.

NOTE: On private property – permission should be sought in advance

99 Museum of Orkney (A6)

Tankerness House, Broad Street, Kirkwall, Orkney

Contains several stones and artifacts dating from the Pictish era, excavated from all over the Orkney islands. (www.orkney.org/museums/tankhouse.htm).

NOTE: [Tel: 01856 873191] Open all year – times vary

P nearby S WC £ Disabled limited access/WC

100 Museum of Scotland (H5)

Chambers Street, Edinburgh

The museum houses the world's largest collection of Pictish artifacts. Many of the most beautiful and famous stones are kept here, along with casts of others. The museum also holds a staggering collection of Dark Age metalwork, including the Pictish hoards found at Norrie's law in Fife and St Ninian's Isle in Shetland.

NOTE: [Tel: 0131 247 4422] Open all year (www.nms.ac.uk)

P nearby S R WC Disabled access/WC

101 Myreton Farm (Picardy Stone) (D6)

NJ 610303   37

In field by minor road off A96, 11 miles SE of Huntly, Aberdeenshire
This 2-metre-tall Class 1 monolith, known as the Picardy Stone, bears a double disc and z-rod, a snake and z-rod and a mirror. In the mid 19th century, a burial was discovered close by. A path to the stone is always kept clear, even when crops are present.
NOTE: Access at all reasonable times

102 Nether Corskie (E6)

NJ 748096   38

In field by minor road off B977, 6 miles SW of Kintore, Aberdeenshire
Probably a prehistoric stone reused by the Picts,

Carved stone – originally from Hilton of Cadboll, but now at the Museum of Scotland. Also see Hilton of Cadboll

the Class 1 stone has a faint carving of a disc and rectangle, and a mirror and comb.
NOTE: On private property – permission should be sought in advance

103 Newton House (D6)

NJ 662297   38

On minor road off B992, 9 miles NW of Inverurie, Aberdeenshire
Erected in the grounds of Newton House around the end of the 19th century, this 2-metre-tall stone shows a double disc above a snake and z-rod. The left-hand disc has a small semicircular notch very deliberately carved into its outline. It stands next to another stone which carries no symbols but does have an Ogham inscription, with the word EDDARRNONN (as at **Brodie Castle**) among the letters. There is also a second inscription written in an unrecognisable script; it has been suggested that these were carved by an illiterate sculptor in imitation of Latin letters.
NOTE: On private property – permission should be sought in advance

104 Nigg Old Parish Church (D5)

NH 805717   21

On minor road off B9175, in Nigg, 7 miles S of Tain, Ross

Standing in Nigg Old Parish Church, this Class 2 cross-slab, although broken with a section missing, is both intricate and exquisite. The front shows a full-length cross, filled with complex interlaced animal designs, surrounded by serpents coiling around intricately worked bosses. Above the cross, fitted into a triangular pediment and carved in high relief, two kneeling figures – representing St Anthony and St Paul in the Syrian desert – receive a loaf of bread from a crow descending from the apex of the slab. The back of the stone carries yet more interlaced designs, surrounding four panels containing: an eagle and a Pictish beast, which is mostly missing; a man armed with spear and sword and carrying a shield pursuing two deer; a figure identified as King David, depicted with a sheep and a harp, rending the lion's jaws; and a mounted huntsman with a hound pursuing a deer, alongside a second man holding two discs. Is this final figure clashing cymbals to startle game, or is he another representation of the double disc?

NOTE: [Tel: 01862 832214] Open Apr-Oct, daily 10.00-17.00 (www.niggoldtrust.org.uk)

105 Pabbay (F1)

NL 607875   31

In graveyard on Pabbay Island, 8 miles SW of Castlebay, Barra

This small stone carries an incised cross, along with a crescent and v-rod and flower symbol. The cross may have been added at a later date.

NOTE: Access at all reasonable times

106 Park House (E6)

NO 780977   38

On minor road off A93, 12 miles SW of Aberdeen, Kincardine & Deeside

In 1821 this stone was taken from Keith's Muir and set up in the grounds of Park House. It shows a crescent and v-rod above a mirror and comb. A third unidentified symbol, possibly a notched rectangle and z-rod, can be found at the top of the stone.

NOTE: On private property – permission should be sought in advance

107 Perth Museum & Art Gallery (G5)

George Street, Perth

The museum holds various exhibits on the history and prehistory of the area, including some Pictish stones, including the St Madoe's cross-slab which is located in the entrance hall, and a stone from Inchyra with both symbols and an Ogham inscription. (www.perthshire.com).

NOTE: [Tel: 01738 632488] Open all year, Mon-Sat 10.00-17.00

P S WC Disabled access/WC

108 Pictavia (F6)

Off A90, Brechin Castle Centre, Brechin, Angus

The fine attraction features information about the Picts, and their enduring legacy, their carved stones. There is a film about the Picts, information about the Battle of Nechtansmere, as well as carved stones, Pictish jewellery and music. Well worth a visit.

NOTE: [Tel: 01307 473765] Open all year, Apr-Sep, Mon-Sat 9.30-17.30, Sun 10.30-17.30; check winter opening (www.pictavia.org.uk)

P S WC £ Disabled access/WC

109 Pitcaple (D6)

NJ 703259 38

On minor road off A96, near Pitcaple, 6 miles NW of Inverurie, Aberdeenshire

There are three Class 1 stones, found on the Moor of Carden and moved here in the 19th century, west of Logie Elphinstone House. The first carries an indecipherable Ogham inscription, along with a crescent and v-rod and double disc and z-rod. The second bears a crescent and v-rod, and a double disc; and the third carries a Pictish beast, and a crescent and v-rod.

NOTE: On private property – permission should be sought in advance

110 Poolewe (D3)

NG 860810 20

In Poolewe churchyard, off A832, in Poolewe, Ross

Not officially recognised until 1994, this is a Class 1 stone bearing a crescent and v-rod.

NOTE: Access at all reasonable times

111 Raasay House (D3)

NG 547368 32

On minor road on island of Raasay, 2 miles N of East Suinish pier

This Class 2 stone was discovered during the building of the road south of Raasay House, and now stands in a rockery in the grounds of the house. It carries a cross set inside a square above a crescent and v-rod.

NOTE: On private property – permission should be sought in advance

Rhynie, Craw Stane

112 Rhynie (Craw Stane) (D6)

NJ 497263 37

In field beside A97, just S of Rhynie, 10 miles S of Huntly, Aberdeenshire
Known as the Craw Stane, this large monolith carries a salmon above a Pictish beast. Seven other carved stones have been found in the area. Two are now located on the village green, one carrying a double disc and z-rod, now almost invisible; and the other showing the remains of a figure holding a spear. Two more have been set up at the entrance to the graveyard: one carries part of a double disc and z-rod, a crescent and v-rod and a mirror; the other bears an animal head beside a vertical double disc and z-rod above a mirror and comb. Two others, including Rhynie Man, can be seen in the **Aberdeenshire Council Offices**. The seventh, which bore a Pictish beast, a crescent and v-rod and a mirror, is now lost.
NOTE: On private property – permission should be sought in advance

113 Rosskeen (D5)

NH 681690 21

In field next to minor road off A9, 1.5 miles W of Invergordon, Ross
This Class 1 monolith is known as the Thief's Stone or *Clach a'Mheirlich*. It carries a stepped rectangle, with a faint crescent and tongs on one side. It can be viewed from the side of the road.
NOTE: On private property – permission should be sought in advance

114 Rossie Priory (G6)

NO 285308   53

On minor road off A90, 7 miles W of Dundee, Angus

The front of this Class 2 cross-slab carries a full-length Celtic cross, beautifully

decorated, although its left arm is now missing. Top left is a four-legged creature with a spiral tail and a human face; below the missing left arm of the cross can be seen a lion-like animal, standing above a man attacked simultaneously by a beast and a fish-tailed serpent; and below this scene are two strange antlered animals, standing upright and facing each other, both gripping a long-necked bird in their jaws. In the top right, a bird-headed human is fighting an unidentified four-legged beast; below,

an animal is trying to swallow a serpent which is laced through its neck and stomach. Beneath this is a very curious creature, like a cross between a lion and a buffalo wearing spectacles; and at the bottom two four-legged beasts with bearded human faces intertwine. On the back is a second ornate cross, although the shaft has been left empty of decoration to accommodate the figures of three mounted men, riding from right to left, one above the other. The topmost horseman is obviously the most important: apart from being the largest, he also has a whole panel to himself. Around the arms of the cross can be seen yet more figures. In the top left is a naked man, holding a pair of birds by their necks; underneath him is a crescent with v-rod, set vertically – perhaps simply to fit into the available space – above a Pictish beast; at the very bottom is a two-headed creature, each head looking at the other. In the top right corner is an angel, whilst below the right-hand arm of the cross there are two more mounted men and a pair of hounds.

NOTE: Stone is housed in a private chapel – permission to view must be obtained in advance

115 Shetland Museum (C7)
Lower Hillhead, Lerwick, Shetland

Although most of the most famous stones, and such archaeological treasures as the St Ninian's Isle hoard, have gone from Shetland to the **Museum of Scotland** in Edinburgh, many more recent finds are on display here, including the eerie Mail figure stone with its wolf-headed man and the Monk's Stone, an early cross-slab from Papil.

NOTE: [Tel: 01595 696729] Usually open all year; curently closed but due to reopen in 2006 (www.shetland-museum.org.uk)

`P nearby`

116 St Andrews Cathedral Museum (G6)
Off A91, in St Andrews, Fife

The museum holds a large collection of sculptured stones, both whole and fragmentary. Pride of place must go to the magnificent St Andrews Sarcophagus, covered with scenes from the life of David carved in high relief. Many other fine stones are in this collection.

NOTE: [Tel: 01334 472563] Open all year; combined ticket available for cathedral and castle

`P nearby  S  £`

117 St Vigeans Museum (G6)
Off A933, 0.5 miles N of Arbroath, Angus

This compact museum houses a fantastic display of sculptured stones, both complete and fragmentary, including the Drosten Stone. This Stone has an Ogham inscription, as well as other carvings of beasts, men and symbols. The collection ranks among the best in the world, and anyone with an interest in Pictish art should go and see it. Highly recommended.

NOTE: [Tel: 01786 450000] Tel to confirm: keys available locally

118 Sandside House (B5)

NC 952652   11

On minor road off A836, 11 miles W of Thurso, Caithness

Now situated in the grounds of Sandside House, this Class 1 stone bears three ovals, a disc and notched rectangle and a mirror and comb.

NOTE: On private property – permission should be sought in advance

119 Scone (G5)

NO 114267   58

Off A93, 2 miles N of Perth

Scone was an important centre of the Picts. It was used by the Kings of Scots, after the union of the Pictish and Scottish kingdoms, from the time of Kenneth MacAlpin in 843, and was the site of inauguration of the Kings of Scots. The Moothill, said to play a part in the ceremony, survives, and the Stone of Destiny was kept here until stolen by Edward I – it is now housed in Edinburgh Castle. Nearby Scone Palace, a 19th-century mansion of the Murrays, is open to the public. (www.scone-palace.net).

NOTE: [Tel: 01738 552300] Open Apr-Oct, daily 9.30-17.30

P S R £ WC   Disabled facilities/WC

120 Shandwick (D5)

NH 855747   21

Off B9166, 4 miles SE of Tain, S of Balintore, Ross

Also known as *Clach a'Charridh*, the Shandwick Stone is an impressive cross-slab encased in a glass box. One side is decorated by a cross made of protruding bosses as well as angels, beasts and interlaced snakes. The other side is divided into five visible panels. Decoration includes a double disc, a Pictish beast, groups of animals, men and riders, and a fine panel of interlacing spirals. The stone was blown down in a gale in 1846 and broken. It was joined back together and re-erected, although it may have been moved from its original position.

NOTE: Access at all reasonable times

121 Strathmiglo (G5)

NO 218102   58

On minor road off A912, 4 miles NW of Falkland, Fife

Now set up at the right hands side of the entrance to the churchyard, this Class 1 stone carries an animal head and a disc and notched rectangle.

NOTE: Access at all reasonable times

122 Strathpeffer Eagle Stone (D4)

NH 485585 26

In field near A834, 5 miles W of Dingwall, Ross

This stone, also known as the Stone of the Turning has many legends associated with it. The Brahan Seer predicted that if the stone fell over three times the Strathpeffer area would be flooded. To date it has fallen twice, and is now – as a precaution – fixed into place. It carries a beautifully carved eagle and an elaborate arch, which some have compared to a horseshoe.

NOTE: Access at all reasonable times

123 Struan Church (F5)

NN 809653 43

On minor road off B847, 5 miles W of Blair Atholl, Perthshire

This broken Class 1 stone bears a double disc and z-rod alongside another obscured symbol and is located in the church, having been found in the burial ground. The churchyard also contains two other carved stones, both carrying incised crosses.

124 Sueno's Stone (D5)

NJ 046595 27 HS

Off A96, on the E edge of Forres, Moray

At over 6 metres high, this is one of the most striking examples of Dark Age sculpture anywhere in Britain, and was probably carved around the 9th century. The west face is

dominated by a huge ring-headed cross, filled with and surrounded by a mass of complex interlace designs. Below the base of the cross, two men bend over a seated central figure, while two smaller figures in the background appear to give benediction. The back of the stone bears 98 separate figures, and although those at the top are worn, all are still plainly visible. The scenes obviously show a battle and the aftermath; depicting fighting, flight and pursuit, headless torsos and lines of bound prisoners. The edges of this thick slab are decorated too, with intertwining foliage, animals, people and monsters.

It has been suggested that this massive stone marks the end of the Pictish period, that it represents a final battle and the triumph of the Scots (although it has been suggested it may commemorate a victory over the Vikings). The seated figure below the cross is said to be Kenneth Mac Alpin – perhaps with the two figures representing Picts and Scots now unified in one king. This is certainly plausible; whatever important event this stone commemorates, it must have been literally monumental.

NOTE: Open all year – stone is enclosed in a glass case for protection – viewing may be difficult in wet weather

P

125 Tarbat Discovery Centre (C5)

Off B9165, in Portmahomack, 11 miles E of Tain, Ross

The visitor centre here has one of the most recently discovered Pictish stones. The stones show a pair of lions fighting over a deer, set above four clerical figures – possibly the four Evangelists – some beautiful spiral designs and a ferocious dragon-like creature with gaping jaws. This stone, along with other items, was found in the ongoing archaeological excavation next to the church, and site tours of the dig are available in the summer months. (www.tarbat-discovery.co.uk).

NOTE: [Tel: 01862 871351] Open Mar-Dec, times vary (a lot)

P S £ **Disabled access difficult but not impossible**

126 Thurso Heritage Museum (B5)

Town Hall, High Street, Thurso, Caithness

This museum houses two fine examples of Class 2 stones from the area.

NOTE: [Tel: 01847 892692] Confirm by tel as appears to be closed at time of writing

Carved stone – now at the Museum of Scotland.

127 Tillypronie House (E6)

NJ 432080 37

On minor road off A97, 8 miles NE of Ballater, Kincardine and Deeside

In the grounds of Tillypronie House, this Class 1 stone displays a crescent and v-rod below a notched rectangle and z-rod.

NOTE: On private property – permission should be sought in advance

128 Trusty's Hill (J4)

NX 588560 83

On hill by minor road off A75, 1.5 miles W of Gatehouse of Fleet, Galloway

A hill-fort, probably in use both before and during the Pictish era, once stood atop this hill. A rock-face next to the entrance carries several carvings, including a double disc and z-rod. There is also a human head with spiralling horns, a sea-monster with a coiled tail and a dagger.

129 Tullich Church (E6)

NO 391975 37

In ruins of Tullich Church, by A93 2 miles E of Ballater, Kincardine and Deeside

Situated within iron railings by the ruins of the old church, this Class 1 stone carries a double disc and z-rod, a Pictish beast, and a mirror.

NOTE: Access at all reasonable times

130 Turriff Manse (D6)

NJ 723499 29

Off A947, in Turriff, Buchan

This broken Class 1 slab is built into the north wall of the old manse garden. It shows part of a crescent and v-rod.

131 Tyrie Church (The Raven Stone) (D6)

NJ 930631   30

On minor road off A98, 5 miles SW of Fraserburgh, Buchan

This Class 1 stone was taken from the foundations of the old church and built into the inside wall of the new. It shows an eagle above a notched rectangle and z-rod.

NOTE: Access at all reasonable times

132 Upper Manbean (D5)

NJ 187576   28

In field next to minor road off B9010, 4 miles S of Elgin, Moray

This Class 1 stone has a piece missing, although it is unclear whether any carving was lost. It carries a sea-monster above a mirror and double-sided comb.

NOTE: On private property – permission should be sought in advance

133 Urquhart Castle (D4)

NH 531286   26   HS

Off A82, 1.5 miles E of Drumnadrochit, Highlands

The Picts had a stronghold here on the banks of Loch Ness. It may be where St Columba confronted a kelpie or beastie – popularly the Loch Ness Monster – and converted the Pictish king Bridei. The site was reused for a medieval castle, substantial remains of which survive, and there is a large new visitor centre. At nearby Drumnadrochit there are two exhibition centres on the Loch Ness Monster.

NOTE: [Tel: 01456 450551] Open all year, daily

P   S   WC   £

134 Whitestones House (D6)

NJ 530470   29

On minor road off B9022, 6 miles N of Huntly, Aberdeenshire

Three Class 1 stones from the surrounding district have been placed in the grounds of Whitestones House. One shows a crescent and v-rod and a double disc and z-rod; the second has the same, except the crescent has no rod; the third has a tall rectangle with a rounded notch in the bottom.

NOTE: On private property – permission should be sought in advance

135 Whithorn Priory & Museum (J4)

NX 444403   83   HS

On A746, in Whithorn, Galloway

The cradle of Christianity in Scotland, Whithorn was founded as a religious centre in the 5th century – and it is from here that St Ninian is said to have converted the southern Picts. Fine collection of early Christian stones, including the Latinus Stone and the Monreith Cross. Managed by the Whithorn Trust.

NOTE: [Tel: 01988 500508] Open Easter-Oct, 10.00-17.00: tel to confirm

P nearby   £

Some other places to visit

Many sites on Hadrian's Wall in Northumberland are open to the public, including the impressive fort at Housesteads [01434 344363] and Chesters, near Hexham [01434 681379], which has a fine bath house. Both are in the care of English Heritage. Parts of the Antonine Wall can also be traced, the best section at Rough Castle (NS 835798), near Bonnybridge.

 Hill forts occupied by the Picts include Dundarg (NJ 895649), Green Castle, Portnockie (NJ 488687), Castle Point, Troup (NJ 838661), Tap o' Noth (NJ 485292), and probably Mither Tap o' Bennachie, near Inverurie (NJ 682223), all in Aberdeenshire. Craig Phaidrig (NH 640452), Highland, may be where St Columba visited and converted the Pictish king Bridei, and excavation has confirmed occupation here in the 6th and 7th centuries. Other confirmed Pictish sites include Burrian, on North Ronaldsay; Buckquoy near the Brough of Birsay – now destroyed by the sea; and Howe, near Stromness, all in Orkney. Clatchard Craig, near Newburgh in Fife, was also used by the Picts but has been destroyed by quarrying. Other strongholds or centres are thought to include Dumyat (NS 832973) and Myothill (NS 782825), both Stirlingshire; Forteviot (NO 052175) and Schiehallion (NN 714548), both Perthshire; Turin Hill (NO 513535) and Finavon Hill (NO 507557), both Angus; and Dunnottar Castle [01569 762173], Kincardine and Deeside. There is a memorial to the Battle of Nechtansmere at Dunnichen (NO 509488).

 Other sites of interest include Edinburgh Castle [0131 225 9846], now home to the Stone of Destiny; as well as Dunstaffnage, Argyll [01631 562465], where the Stone was once kept and a stronghold of Dalriada, the site now occupied by a medieval castle. Dunollie, Oban (NM 852314) was also a stronghold of Dalriada, was destroyed in 698, and the site is also now occupied by a medieval castle.

 Fine examples of early stone crosses include the Kildalton Cross, Islay (NR 458508); Ruthwell Cross, Dumfriesshire (NY 100682); Barochan Cross, Paisley Abbey (NS 485639); Netherton Cross, Hamilton (NS 723555); and the Camus Stone, Panmure House, Angus (NO 519379). Other cross-slabs include that at Crieff (NN 868217). Collections of sculptured stones, with early examples, include those at Keills Chapel, Argyll (NR 691805) and Kilmory Knap, Argyll (NR 702751); and Kirkmadrine, Galloway (NX 080483).

Carved stone, Raasay House

Index